do it **NOW** *do it* **FAST** *do it* **RIGHT**™

Trim

Transformations

do it NOW *do it* FAST *do it* RIGHT™

Trim
Transformations

The Taunton Press

The Taunton Press
Inspiration for hands-on living®

The Taunton Press, Inc., 63 South Main Street, PO Box 5506, Newtown, CT 06470-5506

e-mail: tp@taunton.com

Distributed by Publishers Group West

TEXT AND PHOTOGRAPHY: Nailhouse Publications

WRITER AND PROJECT MANAGER: David Schiff

SERIES EDITOR: Tim Snyder

SERIES DESIGN: Lori Wendin

LAYOUT: Sue Lampe-Wilson

ILLUSTRATOR: Melanie Powell

PHOTOGRAPHER: Stephen Carver

COVER PHOTOGRAPHERS: (front cover) main photo by Scott Gibson, courtesy *Fine Homebuilding*,
© The Taunton Press, Inc.; small photos © Stephen Carver; (back cover) top three photos
© Stephen Carver; bottom photos left to right © Randy O'Rourke

Taunton's Do It Now/Do It Fast/Do It Right™ is a trademark of
The Taunton Press, Inc., registered in the U.S. Patent and Trademark Office.

LIBRARY OF CONGRESS CATALOGING-IN-PUBLICATION DATA
Trim transformations.
     p. cm. -- (Do it now/do it fast/do it right)
  ISBN 1-56158-671-4
  1. Trim carpentry. I. Taunton Press. II. Series.
TH5695.T74 2004
694'.6--dc22
                        2003023782

Printed in the United States of America
10 9 8 7 6 5 4 3 2 1

The following manufacturers/names appearing in *Trim Transformations* are trademarks: Black & Decker®; Bosch™;
Delta®; DeWalt®; Elmer's®; PL® Premium; Porter Cable®; Stanley®; Titebond®.

Acknowledgments

We're grateful to the manufacturers who contributed to this book, including: CST/Berger, Dewalt Industrial Tool Company, Porter-Cable Corporation, Robert Bosch Power Tool Corp., Stanley Tools, and Style Solutions, Inc. Thanks also to the homeowners in and around Warwick, New York, where many of the projects were completed.

Contents

TRIM PROJECTS

Colonial Casing 24
Passageways are important! Use some CLASSIC CASING to dress up the transition between rooms

Elegant & Easy Passageway 34
Hark back to the Victorian era with corner BLOCKS, plinth blocks & FLUTED casing

Building a Better Baseboard 44
This THREE-PIECE TRIM treatment is a lot easier to install than it looks

Post & Lintel 54
Even BUTT JOINTS can be beautiful. This easy trim treatment has plenty of variations you can try

How to Use This Book

I F YOU'RE INTERESTED IN HOME IMPROVEMENTS that add value and convenience while also enabling you to express your own sense of style, you've come to the right place. **Do It Now/Do It Fast/Do It Right** books are created with an attitude that says "Let's get started!" and an ideal mix of home improvement inspiration and how-to information. Do It Now books don't skip important steps or force you to guess at what needs to be done to take a project from start to finish.

You'll find that this book has a friendly, easy-to-use format. (See the sample pages opposite.) You'll begin each project knowing exactly what tools and gear you'll need, and what materials to buy at your home center or building supply outlet. You can get started confidently because every step is illustrated and explained. Along the way, you'll discover plenty of expert advice packed into the margins. For ideas on how to personalize your project, check out the design options pages that follow the step-by-step instructions.

WORK TOGETHER

If you like company when you go to the movies or clean up the kitchen, you'll probably feel the same way about tackling home improvement projects. The work will go faster, and you'll have a partner to share in the adventure. You'll

Get the TOOLS & GEAR you need. You'll also find out what features and details are important.

DO IT RIGHT tells you what it takes to get top-notch results.

DO IT FAST saves you time and trouble.

Know exactly WHAT TO BUY. This list of materials and project supplies will get you in and out of the home center without wasting time.

COOL TOOL puts you in touch with tools that make the job easier.

see that some projects really call for another set of hands to help hold parts in place or steady a ladder. Read through the project you'd like to tackle and note where you're most likely to need help.

PLANNING AND PRACTICE PAY OFF

Most of the projects in this book can easily be completed in a weekend. But the job can take longer if you don't pay attention to planning and project preparation requirements. Check out the conditions in the area where you'll be working. Sometimes repairs are required before you can begin your project. For help, check out the basic techniques in Prep Projects (p. 14). Get Set (p. 4) will tell you about the tools and materials required for most of the projects in this book.

Your skill and confidence will improve with every project you complete. But if you're trying a technique for the first time, it's wise to rehearse before you "go live." This means ordering a little extra in the way of supplies and materials, and finding a location where you can practice your technique.

DESIGN OPTIONS Complete your project with different dimensions, finishes, and details. Explore design options to personalize your project.

DO IT RIGHT tells you what it takes to get top-notch results.

STEP-BY-STEP pages get you started and keep you going to finish the job.

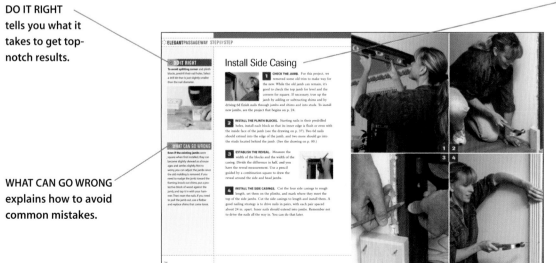

WHAT CAN GO WRONG explains how to avoid common mistakes.

Get Set

Learn the **LINGO**, gather your **GEAR** & learn what to look for
in the **MOLDING** aisle at your local home center or lumberyard

TRIM TRANSFORMATIONS are fun and satisfying. With the right supply of molding, a few tools, and a little know-how, you can add character and detail to an ordinary room. There's no heavy lifting to be done, and you'll save major amounts of money by installing trim yourself. With so many types, styles, and trim materials to choose from, you can get the proportions and details that suit your sense of style, whether you're re-trimming a window, installing wainscot paneling, or embellishing the top of your

walls with a shapely crown molding. To get started, let's cover some useful trim terminology, get the right gear together, and see what moldings are made of.

Trim Terminology

KNOWING WHAT TO LOOK FOR makes all the difference when you arrive at the molding section of your local lumberyard or home center. Don't spend too much time worrying about the difference between trim and molding. These terms have been used interchangeably for years. What's more important is to decide what type of molding you need for your project, what profile looks best, and what material you want your trim to be made of. Molding and trim pieces are named based on how and where they will be installed. A 1x6 board, for example, can become a door jamb or a baseboard. Here's a rundown of the parts you'll be working with.

CORNICE. This molding creates an attractive transition between wall and ceiling. It's usually done with hollow crown molding. (Cornice projects begin on pp. 90 and 98.)

CHAIR RAIL. This horizontal band of molding is usually located about one-third of the way up the wall, and it extends all the way around a room, turning corners and butting into window trim along the way. Chair rail is often seen in dining rooms where it serves the practical purpose of protecting walls from wayward chairs. (See p. 78 for chair-rail installation details.)

WAINSCOT. This trim treatment is for the lower part of the wall, but it can extend to just about any height short of the ceiling. Wallpaper can form a wainscot, but more often, more durable boards or panels are used as shown on p. 65. A wainscot typically is topped with a cap molding and can incorporate other trim details, such as a base cap, baseboard, and shoe. (See p. 44.)

BASEBOARD. This trim detail does just what the name suggests, serving as a transition between wall and floor. A single flat board can be used as baseboard trim, but many

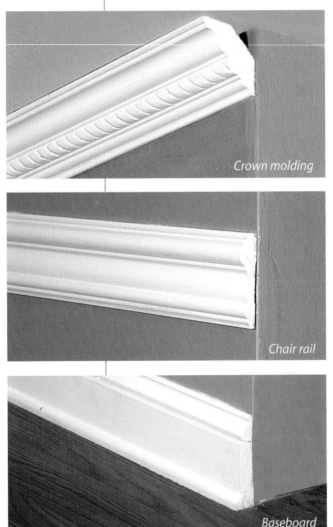

Crown molding

Chair rail

Baseboard

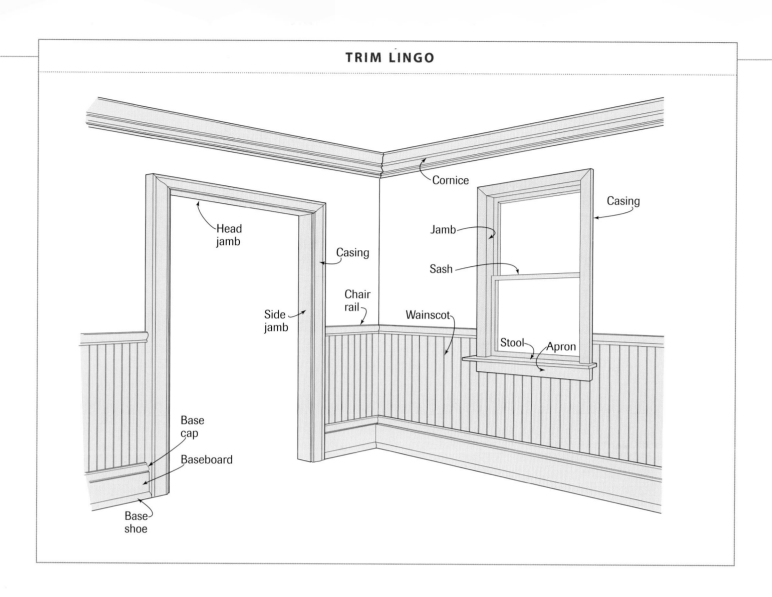

builders like to use a board with a molded detail along the top edge. The most traditional approach is to use a flat baseboard with separate cap and shoe moldings.

SHOE. This thin, flexible molding covers any gaps between the bottom of the baseboard and the floor.

JAMBS. These flat boards finish the inside of a door or window opening.

CASING. Used around windows and doors, casing makes the transition between wall and jamb. The side casing is a vertical piece; the head or top casing runs along the top of the opening.

STOOL. Often mistaken for the sill, the stool is the inside piece that a window closes against.

APRON. This fits under the stool. It's typically made of the same molding as the casing.

▶ DO IT RIGHT

It's a good idea to buy your molding at least two days in advance and store it in the room you will be working in. Unwrap your molding if it comes wrapped in plastic. This will give the material a chance to acclimate to the room's normal temperature and humidity. Don't store trim by leaning it against the wall. Instead, stack your pieces flat on the floor.

The Right Stuff

WHAT SHOULD MY MOLDING BE MADE OF? Once upon a time, there was really only one answer to that question—solid wood—but today there are many more choices. Sure, solid wood is still popular. But other materials are also worth considering. Check out all your options:

SOLID WOOD

Pine is the most common softwood used to make solid-wood molding. It's normally painted but can also be stained or varnished. The same goes for poplar, a common hardwood used to make molding. Oak molding, also common, typically is stained and varnished or just varnished.

FINGER-JOINTED WOOD

Less expensive than solid-wood molding, finger-jointed versions look just as good when they're painted, and this type of wood trim is more resistant to warping and twisting. Want to save time? If so, you can buy finger-jointed moldings already primed and ready for final coats of paint.

FIBERBOARD

Medium-density fiberboard (MDF) is made from wood fiber. MDF is used to make a limited selection of molding profiles. It costs less than solid wood and looks great when painted. Because MDF is denser than wood, you'll want to predrill nail holes to prevent the material from puckering up around the nail. Or save time and install this trim using a power nailer.

FOAM

It may seem strange, but urethane foam is a great material for making moldings (see p. 98). It's lighter than wood and just as easy to cut. It won't

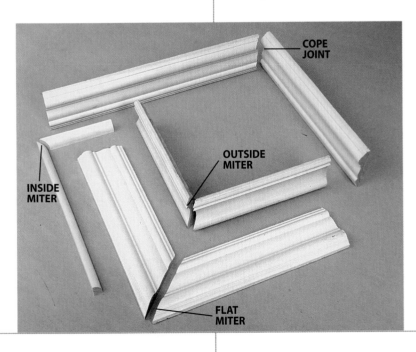

COPE JOINT

OUTSIDE MITER

INSIDE MITER

FLAT MITER

Most of the joints you'll learn to make throughout this book are miters or copes. Outside miters are used whenever molding wraps around an outside wall. For most inside corners, it's best to use a cope joint. Reserve inside miters for very narrow moldings such as base shoe. Flat miters, angled across the face of a board, are used for door and window casings.

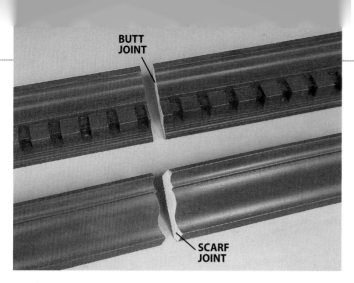

BUTT JOINT

SCARF JOINT

You have two choices if you must use more than one piece of molding to span the length of a wall. One is to cut the pieces square on the end and butt them together. This is the recommended method for polyurethane foam molding. But with wood or MDF molding, it's best to make an angled scarf joint, where pieces meet each other.

warp, bow, or split. And it can be manufactured in a wide variety of sizes and shapes, including some of the most detailed profiles you'll find.

JOINERY DETAILS

You have to know a bit about woodworking joints to tackle trim projects. Get to know the difference between the joints described below and you're well on your way.

BUTT JOINTS are the simplest. The joining parts butt together, so it just takes a couple of square cuts to make a butt joint.

MITER JOINTS are used to join picture frames together and to run trim around an outside corner.

COPE JOINTS are tricky to cut, but fortunately they're only required where trim has to extend around inside corners. In a cope joint, the first piece simply butts into the corner. Then the second piece is cut (coped) to follow the profile of the installed piece.

SCARF JOINTS are used where identical molding pieces have to join each other in a straight run. You create the overlapping scarf joint by making complementary angle cuts in joining pieces.

From the top: urethane foam, MDF, solid wood, finger-jointed wood.

No basic tool kit is complete without a pair of safety glasses. Whenever you use power tools to cut or shape wood, there is always the potential for a splinter to shoot at your eye. Normal prescription glasses don't protect your eyes from the sides, so if you wear prescription glasses, wear safety glasses over them.

▶ **DO IT RIGHT**

As your tool collection grows, you'll need to keep it organized. One good approach is to store tools that tend to get used together in the same milk crate. Grab the crate you need for a particular job. The crates are great as step stools or as an impromptu seat when you want to take a break to admire your work.

Begin with Basic Hand Tools

BUY THEM AS YOU NEED THEM. And when you do buy hand tools, buy the best you can afford. That's the smart approach to building a tool collection. Every project in this book describes the specific tools you'll need for that project. On this page, we'll look at the basic bunch of hand tools you'll need for typical trim projects.

HAMMER & NAIL SET

For trim work, use a 16-oz. hammer with a curved claw. You'll find handles in wood, metal, or fiberglass—it doesn't matter which you choose as long as the handle is firmly attached. Some wood hammers swell out a bit about one-third of the way up to provide a comfortable grip when you have to "choke up." You'll need a nail set to "set" finish nails below the surface so you can then fill the holes with wood putty. Nail sets are available in several tip sizes, but the 1/32-in. tip is fine for most trim projects. The narrow tip fits in a dimple in the top of a finish nail.

MEASURING & LAYOUT TOOLS

Here are the tools you'll need to determine exactly how long pieces should be and exactly where they need to be cut.

TAPE MEASURE. Get a 25-ft. "tape." A good tape will stretch out quite a few feet without collapsing. This makes it easier to measure longer distances without a helper.

A 25-ft. tape measure with a wide, sturdy steel tape will make it easy to measure quickly and accurately.

A good miter box is essential for making tight joints in trim.

COMBINATION SQUARE. Use this tool to lay out 90-degree and 45-degree cut lines. The sliding rule makes it perfect for scribing lines parallel to the edge of a board, as when you're laying out rip cuts or casing reveals (see LINGO on p. 26).

True to its name, a combination square will lay out cut lines at 90 degrees and 45 degrees. It's also great for marking cut lines parallel to an edge.

MITER BOX

To cut exact miters and other joints in pieces of molding, you'll need a good miter box. Look for a model that has the saw supported and guided by a frame. Cheaper plastic and wooden ones use slots to guide the blade and usually produce cuts that aren't as smooth.

Choose a hammer that feels comfortable in your hand—it will be your constant companion. The nail sets shown here have rubber grips that keep your fingers from getting sore after a day of setting nails. The grips are color-coded for tips of three sizes.

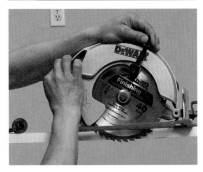

When cutting with a circular saw, adjust cutting depth so the teeth will extend about ½ in. through the bottom of the board. Always unplug the saw when adjusting.

+ SAFETY FIRST

Working safely with power tools will also enable you to work accurately and efficiently. Follow these guidelines:

• Read the owner's manual. Get familiar with a tool's controls and features before you operate it.

• Don't wear loose clothing.

• Protect your eyes and ears. Wear safety glasses or eyeglasses with shatterproof lenses. When using a power saw, use protective plugs or muffs.

• Always unplug your tool when you are making adjustments, changing blades, or changing bits.

• Use only bits and blades that are sharp, in good condition, and designed for use in your saw or drill.

• Make sure that the workpiece is securely supported before you begin cutting or drilling.

• Practice on scrap stock first. Making precise cuts will help you make safe, accurate cuts.

Power Tools for Trim

BRING ON THE POWER! With a few well-chosen power tools, you'll save tons of time on most trim projects. And with a little practice, you'll find that power tools make it possible to get the same smooth, precise results that the pros produce. In addition to the basic selection of power tools described here, you'll find some specialty tools you might also consider using for different projects. When you shop for a new power tool, get one that feels comfortable in your hands and has controls that are easy to operate.

A 12-volt cordless drill/driver has all the power you need for trim work. The best models have variable-speed control and an adjustable clutch.

Use a circular saw for cutting trim boards that are too wide for your miter box or chopsaw. For smooth results, put a carbide-tipped, finish-cutting blade on your saw.

CORDLESS DRILL/DRIVER

This boring tool is anything but dull. On trim projects, you'll use a cordless drill/driver to predrill holes for nails and screws and to drive screws. There's a staggering selection of battery-powered drills available, so if you spend some time in the drill aisle at your home center, you're certain to find a model that feels comfortable to hold and operate. Twelve volts will give you plenty of power. Make sure to get a spare battery for your drill/driver and a kit of basic drill and screwdriver bits, including a couple of countersink bits.

PORTABLE CIRCULAR SAW

Pick out this workhorse carefully. You want a tool that's light but powerful, with a sturdy cast base, depth and angle adjustments that are easy to make, and handles that are comfortable to hold. Ignore horsepower ratings and look for a saw with a 12-amp or 13-amp motor.

CHOPSAW

A chopsaw is a motorized miter box—a circular saw that pivots down to make cuts quickly and precisely. The saw is mounted on a base that swivels, so you can cut just about any angle. If you want to graduate from cutting molding by hand to making miters like the pros do, basic chopsaws sell for around $80. Make sure to equip yours with a carbide-tipped blade designed for finish cuts.

A chopsaw will cut through a piece of molding faster than you can say, "I cut that!" The model shown here runs on a 24-volt battery.

Prep Projects

You'll work faster & better if you prepare your
WALLS, your **TRIM** & your **SAW**

THE AMOUNT OF PREP WORK YOU NEED to do depends on what your space is like and what you're installing. First, you need to get rid of any old trim without damaging the wall. If your trim will be a different color than the walls, you'll save tons of work by giving it a coat of primer and one coat of paint before you install it. The final paint coat blends everything together after you install the trim, caulk the joints, and fill the nail holes. And finally, you'll work faster and better if you assemble the workstation featured here. It holds your miter saw at a comfortable height while supporting long pieces for cutting. The workstation is simple to build from a few pieces of lumber and some screws.

OUT WITH THE OLD   **PAINT PREP**   **FINISHING UP**   **READY FOOTWORK**

Usually, when you remove old molding, there will be a ridge of dried caulk left behind. That's when you'll reach for the razor blade scraper. This inexpensive little tool holds and retracts single-edged razor blades. It's designed to remove dried paint from window glass, but it also does a great job of zipping off that caulk ridge.

Before you install new trim and give the room fresh coats of paint, you'll want to repair any nail holes or dents in the walls. Depending on the size of the damage, use a putty knife or 6-in. drywall knife to fill the holes with spackling compound. When the compound hardens, sand the repair smooth with the wall surface using 80-grit sandpaper.

Remove Old Trim

1 **BREAK THE SEAL.** In most cases, the edges of your old trim will be sealed to the drywall with a bead of caulk and layers of paint that have been applied over the years. If you try to remove the trim without breaking the seal first, you will most likely rip the top layer of paper off

the drywall surface. To break the seal, put a new blade in your utility knife. Insert the knife between the trim and wall, and carefully cut through the paint and caulk. It might take three or four passes, depending on how many layers of paint you have to cut through.

2 **PULL THE TRIM AWAY FROM THE WALL.** Grab a 6-in. drywall-finishing knife, and tap it with your hammer to wedge it between the trim and the wall. Do this in several places along the trim. The idea is to create just enough space to get your flatbar started.

3 **PRY OFF THE TRIM.** Place the blade of your flatbar between the wall and the trim, then protect the wall with a piece of ¼-in.-thick plywood. Gently pry the molding away at several spots until you can see where the nails are. Now position the bar and plywood near each nail, and pry the molding farther away from the wall until you can easily pull it off.

4 **REMOVE THE NAILS.** Whether or not you intend to save the old trim, get in the habit of removing the nails before you put down each piece—trim with nails sticking out is very dangerous. The easiest way to remove nails is to use end nips to pry them out through the back of the molding. This also prevents damage to the face of the molding in case you intend to reuse it.

Prefinish the Trim

1 **APPLY A COAT OF PRIMER.** Lay your trim pieces across two saw-horses to work at a convenient height. To protect the floor from drips, put newspaper or a dropcloth under the horses. Give the trim a coat of latex primer, working the primer into the wood by brushing back and forth. If any drips get on the back of the trim, wipe them off—it's annoying to scrape off dried drips so that the trim can lay flat against the wall.

2 **APPLY THE FIRST COAT OF PAINT.** The job will be easier and neater if you pour a few inches of paint into a separate bucket instead of working out of the paint can. Dip your brush about one-third of the way into your paint bucket, and lightly tap it twice against the sides to prevent drips. Apply the paint in long, smooth strokes.

Caulk, Fill & Paint

1 **CAULK & FILL.** Even if you manage to install trim without gaps, it's still a good idea to run a bead of paintable latex caulk at joints and where trim meets the wall. The trim may shrink, and caulk is flexible enough to prevent future gaps. Work the caulk in with a wet finger, then smooth with a wet sponge or paper towel. Fill nail holes with wood putty and sand.

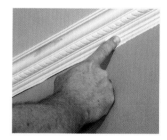

2 **APPLY THE LAST PAINT COAT.** For top coats, 100% acrylic trim paint in a semigloss sheen is a good choice. Use a quality brush to apply the final coats of paint to the molding. If you plan to paint the wall, you can let your trim coat extend onto the wall surface. You'll paint over this extra finish when applying wall paint.

◆ DO IT NOW

Here's a list of materials you'll need to gather before you start building your workstation:

- One 8-ft. 2x4
- One 10-ft. 2x6
- Twenty-four 3-in.-long coarse-threaded drywall screws
- To attach a chopsaw—four ⅜-in.-dia. by 3-in. machine bolts with eight washers, four lock washers, and four wing nuts
- To attach a hand miter box—four 1¼-in. drywall screws

For the sawhorses:

- Four 8-ft. 2x4s
- One set of sawhorse brackets
- Thirty-two 1¼-in. drywall screws

✳ WHAT'S DIFFERENT?

You'll see them sold as drywall screws, deck screws, or all-purpose screws. They all have a sharp point and aggressive thread designed to be power-driven quickly and easily into wood. Drywall screws typically are black and also are available with a finer thread for attaching drywall to metal studs. Deck screws are coated to prevent rust in outdoor applications. From left: a coarse-thread screw, a fine-thread screw, and a coated deck screw.

Build a Miter-Saw Workstation

1 **ASSEMBLE THE SAWHORSES.** As shown in step 8 on p. 23, the workstation will fit on any pair of sawhorses with 2x4 crosspieces. If you need to make a pair, cut two 2x4 crosspieces 32 in. long and eight legs 30 in. long. Assemble the sawhorses, driving 1¼-in. screws through the sawhorse brackets into the legs and crosspieces.

2 **CUT THE 2X4 SUPPORTS & CLEATS.** The front of your saw will sit on the 10-ft. 2x6. Cut a 45-in. length of 2x4 to support the back of your saw. Pairs of 2x4 cleats hold the supports on the sawhorses. Cut four 2x4 cleats 3½ in. long and two that are 5½ in. long.

3 **LAY OUT THE CLEAT POSITIONS.** As shown in step 8 on p. 23, the 45-in. 2x4 support and the 10-ft. 2x6 support both require short cleats that straddle the sawhorse. Clamp the 2x4 and 2x6 supports together with their centers aligned and use your square to lay out

cleat locations. Extend layout lines down one side of each support piece.

4 **ATTACH THE CLEATS.** Clamp each cleat in place between its layout lines, check that it is square to the 2x6, and drive two 3-in. screws through the 2x6 into the cleat. Do the same for the 2x4 support. Nice work so far. Get your supports set up on the sawhorses.

Attach Blocks & the Saw

5 **DRILL FOR BOLT HOLES.** If you have a power miter saw, you'll attach and remove it quickly and without tools using ⅜-in. bolts and wing nuts. Center the saw across the 2x6 support, flush to the front. Adjust the back of the 2x4 flush to the back of the saw. Using a  ⁷⁄₁₆-in.-dia. drill bit, bore through the holes in the saw base and into the supports. You can remove the saw to complete the holes. Put the saw back in place and bolt it down, using a washer at the top and a washer, lock washer, and wing nut at the bottom.

 **6** **CUT SUPPORT BLOCKS.** Four blocks, two attached to each side of the 2x6, support long pieces during cutting. To determine the length of your blocks, measure from the front of the 2x6 to the saw fence and add about an inch—7 in. worked for the saw shown here. Cut a piece of 2x4 long enough to make all four blocks.

The blocks must be at the same height as your saw table. Place the 2x4 you just cut against the table, and mark the height. Rip-cut the 2x4 to this width, then cut it into four blocks.

7 **ATTACH SUPPORT BLOCKS.** Attach two of the support blocks near the ends of the 2x6 by clamping them in place and then driving 3-in. screws up through the bottom. In the same way, attach the other two blocks 14 in. from each side of the saw.

8 **GO TO WORK.** Okay, now you're set up like a pro to cut some trim. You'll find yourself using this station for other tasks too—supporting workpieces for predrilling or cutting cope joints, for example. So go to it. Take your time, remember your safety glasses, and, most of all, enjoy the experience of making your home a more beautiful place to live.

5

6

7

8

Colonial Casing

Passageways are important! Use some **CLASSIC CASING** to dress up the transition between rooms

MANY NEWER HOMES HAVE NOTHING more than drywall surrounding passageways between rooms. Fortunately, trimming out these openings is easy. And since our eyes are drawn to passageways, creating an attractive room transition will add lots of architectural impact.

This project features mitered corners. Think of the casing as a large-scale picture frame that allows the molding's profile to wrap around the opening. You can also add style to a passageway using corner blocks and fluted casing (see p. 34) or with a post-and-lintel treatment (see p. 54). No matter which treatment you choose, the techniques shown here will give you first-class results.

| MEASURE | INSTALL THE JAMBS | LAY OUT THE REVEAL | INSTALL THE CASINGS |

⠿ LINGO

When installing casing around an opening, don't completely cover the edge of the jambs. Instead, leave a "reveal" about 1/8 in. wide. Believe it or not, this little ledge makes a big difference in the project's final appearance.

❖ COOL TOOL

A rip guide is a circular saw accessory that costs little but helps a lot. The guide fits into slots in the saw's base and has a short fence that rides against the edge of the board you're cutting. You can adjust the guide to rip boards of different widths. Make sure the guide you buy is sized to fit your saw.

Tools & Gear

Keep your basic tool kit handy because you'll need a hammer, tape measure, and nail set, as well as the tools listed below.

CIRCULAR SAW. This is the tool you'll use to cut the wood jambs that will line the inside of the passageway. To help you cut straight, fit your saw with a rip guide (see COOL TOOL at left).

DRILL & BIT. A cordless drill is fine for this project. You'll need a 1/16-in.-dia. bit to go with it.

MITER BOX. Since good miter joints are important here, make sure you have a good-quality miter box or a chopsaw. Both tools will give you the exact 45-degree cuts this project requires.

COMBINATION SQUARE. Thanks to its adjustable blade, this square is great for marking the reveal lines on your jambs (see LINGO at left).

FRAMING SQUARE. With its long blades, this tool makes it easy to test door openings for square.

FOUR-FOOT LEVEL. You'll need a 4-ft. level to make sure your head jamb is level and your side jambs are plumb. Use a 2-ft. level for narrower openings.

SAWHORSES. Set up a pair of horses and a 2x10 or 2x12 crosspiece to support your miter box. Or make yourself the miter-saw stand described on p. 20.

STEPLADDER OR STOOL. One is essential. If you're working with a helper, get two ways to step up and you'll have an easy time installing the top casing.

CAULKING GUN. Have your gun ready as you near the end of the project, so you can seal small cracks in preparation for painting.

TRIM BRUSH. If you've completed other projects in this book, you already know how important a good trim brush can be. A brush that's about 3 in. wide offers the best combination of control and painting speed.

What to Buy

1| JAMB STOCK. For this project, you'll need to cut a head jamb and two side jambs to line the inside of the passageway. Measure your opening and get three pieces of 1x6 pine, giving yourself a few extra inches on each piece. Buy only boards that are flat and straight. We used preprimed pine for this project to save time on painting.

2| MOLDING. If you spend some time in the molding aisle at your home center, you're sure to find a pleasing casing profile. There are quite a few choices. The casing we used is 3 in. wide and comes preprimed. Assuming your passageway opening is around 7 ft. tall, you'll need to buy four 8-ft. pieces (for side casings) and two head casing pieces at least 12 in. longer than the width of the opening.

3| SHIMS. You'll probably need shims to make the head casing level and the side casings plumb. Buy a small package of tapered wood shims.

4| FINISH NAILS. Get some 8d finish nails for installing jambs and 6d finish nails for the trim.

5| CAULK & WOOD PUTTY. Acrylic latex caulk is the best stuff to use for filling gaps in joints and between the molding and the wall. To fill nail holes, get wood putty.

6| SANDPAPER. Several sheets of 120-grit sandpaper should handle the smoothing work you'll need to do prior to painting.

7| PAINT & PRIMER. Use a fast-drying interior primer and good-quality semigloss trim paint.

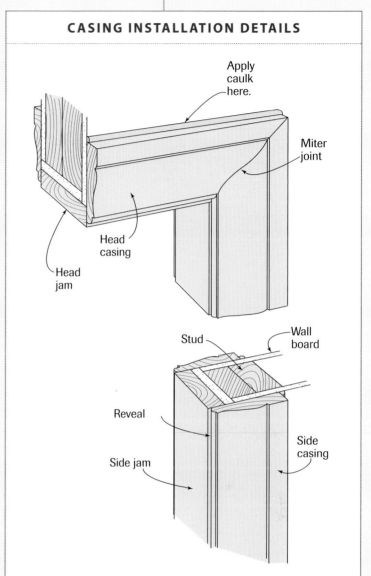

CASING INSTALLATION DETAILS

Apply caulk here.

Miter joint

Head casing

Head jam

Stud

Wall board

Reveal

Side casing

Side jam

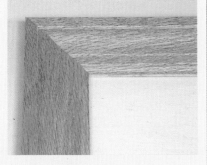
Prepare the Jamb

1 **CHECK FOR SQUARE, STRAIGHT & PLUMB.**
If the existing opening isn't true, you'll need to insert shims beneath your jambs to make the opening square and get surfaces plumb and level. Put a framing square in each corner to see if it's out of square. Then use your  4-ft. level to check both sides of the opening for plumb and the top of the opening for level. Mark where you think your new jambs will need to be shimmed out.

2 **MEASURE FOR JAMB WIDTH.** It's important to cut your jambs about ⅛ in. wider than the wall thickness. This ensures that your molding will lie flat against the wall. Drywall-finished openings in most houses are about 4¾ in. thick. Measure wall thickness in several places, and add ⅛ in. to the largest width you get.

3 **RIP YOUR JAMBS TO WIDTH.** Mark a piece of 1x6 jamb stock to the width you need. With your circular saw unplugged, adjust the saw's rip guide so you'll be cutting your jambs to the right width. Not sure? No problem. Rip a test piece of scrap wood, and see if it measures up. When you know the setting is right, rip all three pieces of jamb stock to width.

4 **CUT & INSTALL THE HEAD JAMB.** Cut the head jamb to length for a snug fit. If the top of the opening came out level (step 1), you can simply nail the jamb against the drywall. If not, insert shims as necessary to bring the bottom face of the jamb into level. Always  insert shims in pairs, from opposite sides of the opening. Make sure the jamb is centered side to side, then drive a pair of 8d finish nails next to the shim. Keep checking for level, add shims in the gap as necessary, and nail about every 24 in.

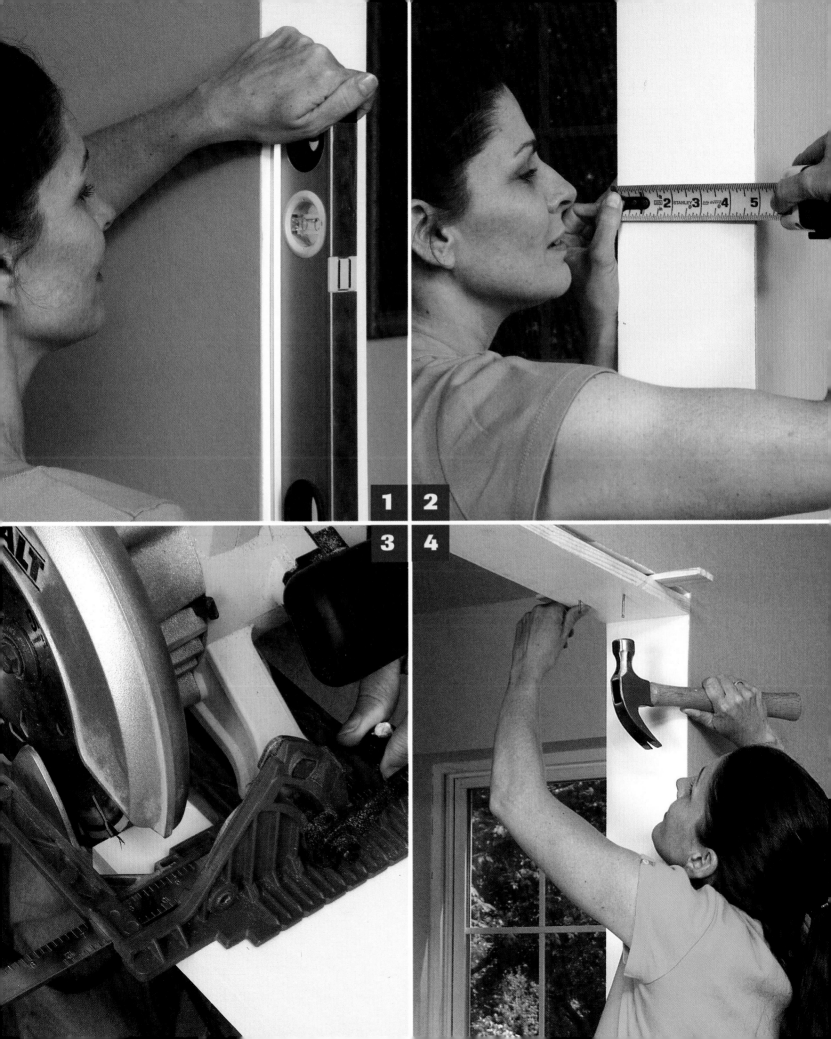

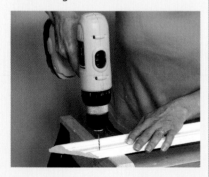

Install the Casing

5 **CUT & INSTALL THE SIDE JAMBS.** Measure from the head jamb to the floor on both sides, and cut a side jamb for each side. Shim one or both jambs if necessary, then install with pairs of 8d nails about every 24 in. Cut the shims off flush with jamb edges, using a utility knife or a handsaw.

6 **LAY OUT THE REVEAL.** To lay out the reveal (see LINGO on p. 26), set a combination square to ⅛ in. Place a pencil in the notch in the end of the square's blade and run the square around the edges of your jambs.

7 **INSTALL THE SIDE CASINGS.** Cut each piece to rough length, and hold it in place against its reveal line. Mark for the miter cut at the top reveal line. Using your combination square, extend the miter line across the molding, then make the cut on your miter saw. Attach each side casing with pairs of 6d nails about every 24 in. Drive one nail into the jamb edge and the other through the drywall into the framing.

8 **INSTALL THE HEAD CASING.** Cut the head casing to rough length and miter-cut one end. Hold the piece upside-down against the wall, with the tip of the miter cut touching the tip of the mating miter. (Have a helper hold the piece if you can't reach both

ends.) This allows you to mark accurately for the remaining miter cut. Cut and install the casing, then take a break. You still need to set nails below the surface, fill holes, caulk joints, sand, and paint. But the toughest carpentry work is done, and your passageway already looks great.

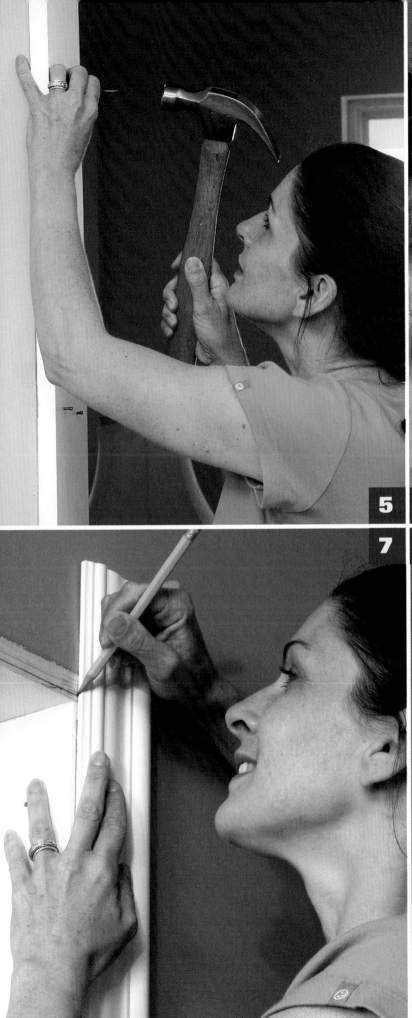
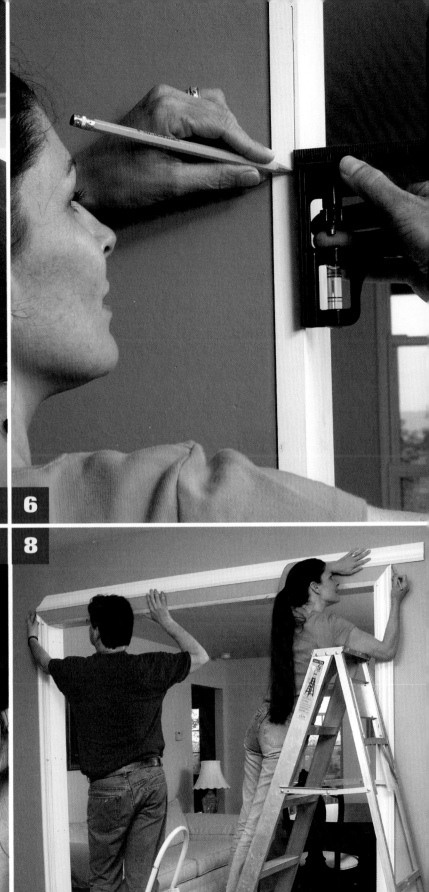

5 **6**

7 **8**

This door casing has Colonial origins and classic staying power. The flat section of the molding lends strength and mass. The outer contours add detail and delicacy.

When the bottom of a window jamb lacks a flat stool, as shown above, the best trim strategy often calls for miter joints at all four corners. The natural finish theme extends to the built-in desk.

Mitered trim treatments that include mitered corners can look great around windows, doors, passageways, and even built-in cabinetry. There are dozens of different molding profiles that look distinctive when their contours are "wrapped" around a corner with well-made miter joints.

Elegant & Easy Passageway

Hark back to the Victorian era with corner **BLOCKS**, plinth blocks & **FLUTED** casing

I T HAD TO BE A CLEVER VICTORIAN trim carpenter who came up with the idea of corner and plinth blocks. He was probably looking for an easier way to install the increasingly ornate door and window casings that are the hallmark of the era. What a great solution! All the pieces meet with butt joints—easier to measure and fit than miters. If you try this trim treatment around a passageway or doorway, consider upgrading your baseboard trim as well (see p. 44). Blocks and flutes also look great around a window.

PLINTH BLOCKS   SIDE CASINGS   HEAD CASINGS   CORNER BLOCKS

▶ LINGO

Like many of our architectural forms, the combination of a plinth block with fluted casing is an interpretation of an ancient Greek architectural style. Flutes were originally carved into round stone columns that sat on a square base called a plinth.

⊙ DO IT RIGHT

A utility knife can do a more accurate job than a pencil of marking something in place—like marking where to cut casing (see step 3 on p. 38). Just deeply nick the molding with the knife. Put the molding on a flat surface, place the blade in the nick, and move the square against the blade to score a cut line onto the molding.

Tools & Gear

Keep your basic tool kit handy because you'll need a hammer, tape measure, and nail set.

DRILL & BIT. To avoid splitting the wood, you'll need to predrill all nail holes in corner blocks and plinths. A corded or cordless drill will do the job, along with a $1/16$-in.-dia. bit.

MITER BOX. To cut perfectly square joints in the casing, you'll need a miter box. Go with a model like the one shown here, which comes with its own fine-tooth blade. If you want pro-level speed and precision, invest in a chopsaw (see p. 13).

FRAMING SQUARE. This big square is for large-sized layout work, like checking a door opening for square.

COMBINATION SQUARE. This adjustable square is a versatile layout tool. For this project, you'll need a combination square to lay out the reveals.

FOUR-FT. LEVEL. A 4-ft. level will help you make sure that your side jambs are plumb. If the head jamb is narrower than 4 ft., you'll need a 2-ft. level too.

CAULKING GUN. You'll use this to dispense the caulk to seal the joint between wall and casing.

STEPLADDER OR STOOL. Unless you have unusually high openings or are short, you only need to get up a step or two to trim an entryway. You can use any stepladder up to 6 ft., but a shorter one will be more convenient. Or grab a stool like the one shown on p. 56 (COOL TOOL).

TRIM BRUSH. Your new trim deserves a nice finish. Apply it with a high-quality trim brush that's about 3 in. wide. If you're using oil-based finish, make sure to get a natural-bristle brush or a synthetic brush recommended for use with oil or alkyd finishes.

BLOCK

FLUTED CASING

PLINTH

What to Buy

1 | CASING, CORNER BLOCKS & PLINTH BLOCKS. Most home centers and lumberyards display corner block, casing, and plinth block combinations that work together. Choose a "set" you like. To complete both sides of a passageway like the one shown here, you'll need four plinth blocks, four corner blocks, and enough casing to make four side casing pieces and two top, or head, casing pieces. The plinth blocks and corner blocks will have fixed dimensions, but you'll cut the casing pieces to fit.

2 | FINISH NAILS. You'll need 6d (2-in.) finish nails to install all parts of this project.

3 | SANDPAPER. Use 120-grit sandpaper to sand putty patches for molding that will be painted.

4 | PUTTY & CAULK. The putty is for filling nail holes. Caulk is for filling gaps between the casing and for filling less-than-perfect joints. Acrylic latex caulk is the type you want.

5 | PRIMER & PAINT. If you plan to paint your molding, use a good-quality primer under two coats of semigloss interior trim paint.

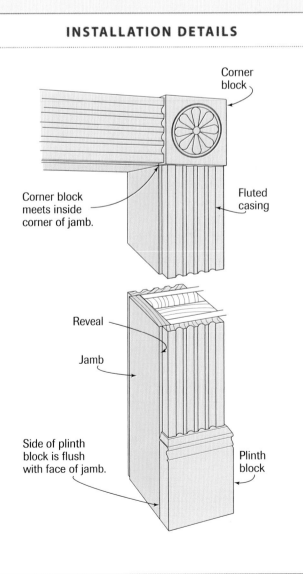

INSTALLATION DETAILS

Corner block

Corner block meets inside corner of jamb.

Fluted casing

Reveal

Jamb

Side of plinth block is flush with face of jamb.

Plinth block

▶ DO IT RIGHT

To avoid splitting corner and plinth blocks, predrill their nail holes. Select a drill bit that is just slightly smaller than the nail diameter.

✚ WHAT CAN GO WRONG

Even if the existing jambs were square when first installed, they can become slightly skewed as a house ages and settles. Not to worry, you can adjust the jambs once the old molding is removed. If you need to nudge the jamb toward the framing, knock out shims, put a protective block of wood against the jamb, and tap it in with your hammer. Then reset the nails. If you need to pull the jamb out, use a flatbar, and replace shims that come loose.

Install Side Casing

1 **CHECK THE JAMB.** For this project, we removed some old trim to make way for the new. While the old jamb can remain, it's good to check the top jamb for level and the corners for square. If necessary, true up the jamb by adding or subtracting shims and by driving 6d finish nails through jambs and shims and into studs. To install new jambs, see the project that begins on p. 24.

2 **INSTALL THE PLINTH BLOCKS.** Starting nails in their predrilled holes, install each block so that its inner edge is flush or even with the inside face of the jamb (see the drawing on p. 37). Two 6d nails should extend into the edge of the jamb, and two more should go into the studs located behind the jamb.

3 **ESTABLISH THE REVEAL.** Measure the width of the blocks and the width of the casing. Divide the difference in half, and you have the reveal measurement. Use a pencil guided by a combination square to draw the reveal around the side and head jambs.

4 **INSTALL THE SIDE CASINGS.** Cut the four side casings to rough length, set them on the plinths, and mark where they meet the top of the side jambs. Cut the side casings to length and install them. A good nailing strategy is to drive nails in pairs, with each pair spaced about 24 in. apart. Inner nails should extend into jambs. Remember not to drive the nails all the way in. You can do that later.

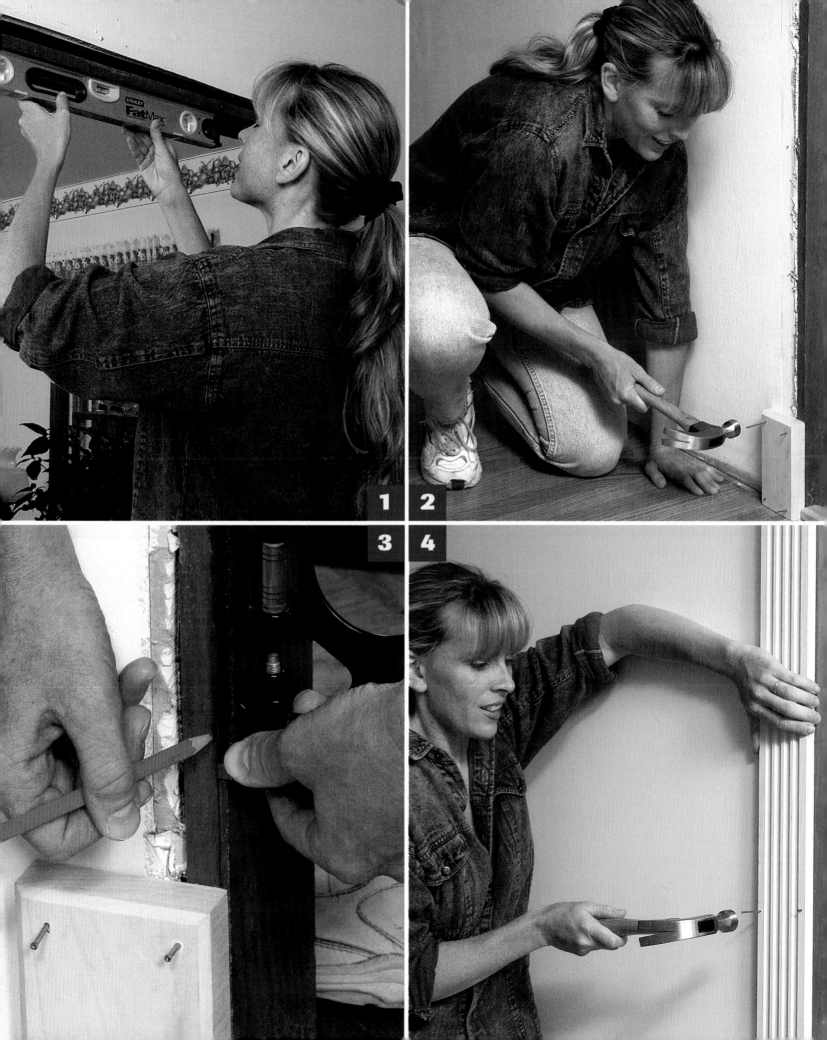

1

2

3

4

As you install casing, drive nails only partway in, just in case you need to make an adjustment later. When all the casing is installed and you are satisfied with the joints, complete the nailing and set the nails.

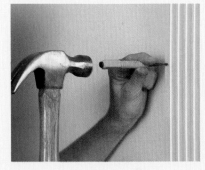

Did you ever get a piece in exactly the right position and then have it slip while you drive the first nail? To avoid this, start the first couple of nails before you position the workpiece. If just the point of the nail is protruding from the back of the workpiece, it's easy to get the piece positioned exactly and keep it that way as you drive your nails.

Finish It Up

5 **INSTALL THE FIRST CORNER BLOCK.** Install one corner block on each side of the opening. Align each block so its bottom corners meet the inside corner of the jamb as shown in the drawing on p. 37. Fasten each block by driving four 6d nails in predrilled holes.

6 **MARK, CUT & INSTALL THE HEAD CASINGS.** Cut one end of each head casing square. Butt the square end against the corner block installed in step 5, and mark the opposite end where it meets the inside corner formed by the head and side jambs. Cut the head casing to fit, then install it by driving 6d nails every 24 in.

7 **INSTALL THE REMAINING BLOCKS.** Next, just butt the remaining blocks into position and nail them in place. As in step 5, you'll want to install each block with four 6d nails, driven in predrilled holes.

8 **FINISH THE JOB.** Easy, wasn't it? Now it's time to caulk where molding meets wall and jamb. Also use your finger to smooth caulk into any gaps between the casing and the blocks. Set all nails, fill the holes with putty, and sand smooth. Apply primer and finish coats of paint.

Who says the corner blocks have to go on the top? In this bathroom, a corner nook presented the opportunity to create an inset display shelf with fluted casing topped with capitals. Corner blocks instead of plinth blocks are used at the bottom. All the moldings in this room are made of polyurethane foam.

Modern media finds a 19th-century-style home in these shallow shelves built into the stud space. Corner blocks with rosettes and fluted casings trim the opening with a Victorian flair.

Proportions are important when you're trimming an opening with corner blocks and casing. That's why these moldings come in different sizes. Whether you're trimming out a door, a window, or a built-in bookcase, blocks and flutes draw attention to the opening or items that they frame.

It's a small door that leads to a bathroom, but it has style, thanks to its trim. Fluted casing, plinth blocks, and corner blocks are painted to match the door and the baseboard moldings. Set against the taupe-colored walls, the effect is elegant yet warm.

Top: Victorian-era trim was often stained a dark tint, as are these modern-day casings. Today, feel free to take liberties with mixing paint colors and stains in the same room.

Bottom: Plinth and corner blocks are available in poplar (right) as well as pine (left). Poplar costs more, but it has a finer grain than pine and looks better when painted.

Building a Better Baseboard

This **THREE-PIECE TRIM** treatment is a lot easier to install than it looks

NOBODY LIKES GETTING STUCK in an ugly pair of shoes. That's why every room in your house deserves a nice baseboard to dress up the bottom of the wall and create a pleasing transition where the floor stops and the wall begins. The three-piece baseboard we're building here is a great upgrade in any room that's hampered by skimpy base molding. And here's something interesting you'll discover when you tackle this project: The three-piece design of the baseboard can actually make it easier to install than some one-piece baseboards, especially if you're dealing with irregular wall and floor surfaces. Let's get started . . .

ROOM & BOARD   MAKING MITERS   COPING SKILLS   FINAL SAND

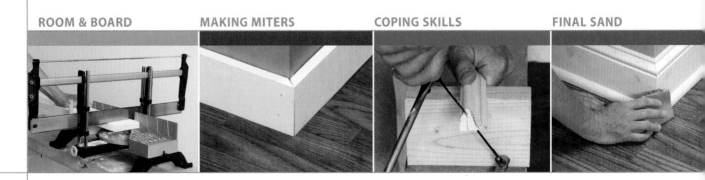

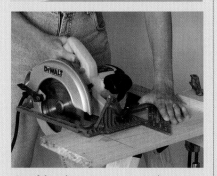

Combination square or angle square? Both work for laying out square or 45-degree angles. The angle square has calibrations for laying out loads of other angles, too. And this thick, durable square also works well as a guide for making square cuts with your circular saw.

The combination square has a ruler that slides in the handle, making it ideal for marking lines and reveals. The best combination squares have a built-in level and a scribing point that stows in the handle.

Tools & Gear

Keep your basic tool kit handy because you'll need a hammer, tape measure, and nail set. Also gather up the tools listed below.

DRILL & BIT. You'll need a corded or cordless drill equipped with a $1/16$-in. bit to predrill nail holes for scarf joints.

MITER BOX. You'll use a miter box to make exact cuts in trim pieces. A good miter box like the one used in this project comes with its own fine-tooth saw and costs about $40.

SQUARE. Either a combination square or an angle square will do. See "What's Different?" at left.

COPING SAW. This small saw has a thin blade designed for cutting curves. You'll need it to cut the cope joints in cap molding pieces. Since these blades break easily, make sure you've got several spare blades on hand.

FILES. With a small, flat file and a tapered, round "rat-tail" file you can fine-tune the fit of your cope joints.

CAULKING GUN. You'll use this to dispense the caulk to seal the joint between wall and casing.

TRIM BRUSH. Your new trim deserves a nice finish. Apply it with a high-quality trim brush that's 2 in. to 3 in. wide. If you're using oil-based finish, make sure to use a natural-bristle brush or a synthetic brush recommended for use with oil or alkyd finishes.

DO IT RIGHT

Look closely at an unfinished board and you may notice a series of ripples running across the surface. These are caused by planer blades during the milling process. When you apply paint or varnish, these surface irregularities can become quite noticeable. That's why it's smart to sand the wood surface smooth before you use a board to trim a room. Start with 80-grit sandpaper, and finish up with 120-grit sandpaper. A belt sander gets the job done quickly, but a random-orbit sander will also work.

What to Buy

2 CAP MOLDING

1 — BASEBOARD

3 SHOE MOLDING

1 **BASEBOARD.** The baseboard will be 1x4, 1x6, or 1x8 (this project used 1x4). You can use either #2 pine or finger-jointed boards that are preprimed (as shown here). To compile your lumber order, measure each wall length and subtract door openings. Add some extra (about 10%) to make sure you'll have enough. You'll need cap molding and shoe molding of the same lengths.

2 **CAP MOLDING.** This molding creates a graceful transition between the baseboard and wall. "Caps" come in several profiles and heights. Find one that looks good on the top edge of your baseboard.

3 **SHOE MOLDING.** Shoe molding closes up the gap between the baseboard and floor. It comes in several thicknesses and heights. Here we used molding that's ½ in. thick at the bottom and ¾ in. high.

4 **FINISH NAILS.** You'll need 8d (2½-in.) finish nails for the baseboard, 4d (1½-in.) nails for the cap, and 1-in. brads for the shoe molding.

5 **SANDPAPER.** Use 120-grit sandpaper to sand putty patches for molding that will be painted.

6 **WOOD GLUE & PUTTY.** Yellow wood glue will be used at miter joints. Putty is for filling nail holes.

7 **CAULK.** Buy a paintable latex acrylic caulk, so you can fill small gaps between the wall and the top of the baseboard.

8 **PRIMER & PAINT.** Use a good-quality primer under two coats of semigloss trim paint.

PLANNING THE JOB

A good prep step for this project is to draw a plan view of the room and identify what lengths of trim you need and which joints go where. For example, all three baseboard trim pieces will butt against a door casing. On inside corners, the two boards simply butt together, while the cap and shoe moldings need to meet with cope joints. On outside corners, all pieces meet each other with miter joints. And along the length of a wall, there should be an angled scarf joint where one piece of molding ends and another joins it to continue the molding run. (For more on joinery details, see pp. 8–9.)

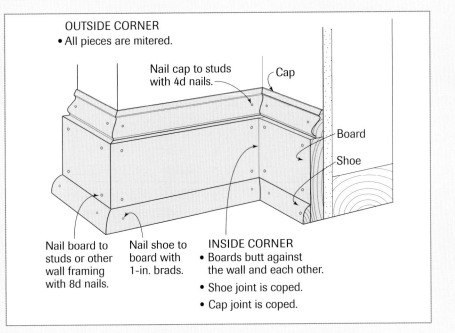

OUTSIDE CORNER
• All pieces are mitered.

Nail cap to studs with 4d nails.

Cap

Board

Shoe

Nail board to studs or other wall framing with 8d nails.

Nail shoe to board with 1-in. brads.

INSIDE CORNER
• Boards butt against the wall and each other.
• Shoe joint is coped.
• Cap joint is coped.

Install the Board

1 **GET THE FIRST BOARD UP!** After marking stud locations on the wall just above where the baseboard will be installed, you can cut and install your first board. Make it a board that simply butts against the wall. If a baseboard heater gets in the way, stop the board about ⅛ in. away from the edge of the unit. Cut the board to length on your miter saw. Install each board by driving two 8d finish nails at each stud location.

2 **INSTALL SOME MORE.** Cut and install as many butt-jointed pieces as you can. If you need more than one board to cover a wall, go to the next step. To mark a board that fits against door casing, try this trick: Make a board-sized notch in a small, rectangular piece of plywood or pine. Put the baseboard in place, letting one end run past the door casing. Hold the jig against the casing and over the board, then mark your cut line along the edge of the jig.

3 **USE SCARF JOINTS AS NEEDED.** If you need to install more than one board along a wall, cut a 45-degree scarf joint like the pros do; it's less noticeable than a butt joint. Try to locate the scarf joint near a stud. Set your miter saw to make a 45-degree cut. Cut and install one board, then the other, taking care to glue and align the joint. Take note: Scarf joints also work for cap and shoe molding.

4 **COMPLETE OUTSIDE CORNERS.** Don't measure for these miter cuts; it's more accurate to hold the board in its installed position and mark the outside miter cut right against the corner of the wall. Use an angle square or a combination square to mark the

miter cut on the edge of the board. Position the board carefully in your miter box so that the entire blade is on the "waste" side of the cut. Install each outside corner as you mark and cut it.

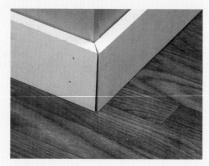
Install Cap & Shoe

5 **INSTALL THE FIRST CAP PIECE.** Square-cut the first piece to fit between two inside corners. Install the cap by driving 1-in. brads into each stud. Try this tip: Angle the nail downward so the cap will be pulled tightly against the top of the board.

6 **COPE THE CAP.** Cut the next cap piece about 6 in. longer than it needs to be. On your miter saw, make a 45-degree cut on the end to be coped as if you were cutting an inside miter joint. Next, cut along this profile with your coping saw. Angle the blade back to

remove all the wood that could stop the profile from fitting tightly against the mating piece. Don't worry if you have to stop cutting in one direction and start cutting in another.

7 **TUNE THE FIT & FASTEN THE PIECE.** Test-fit the cope against a scrap of cap. Using a file, fine-tune the fit of the joint. When it's right, measure, mark, and cut the cap piece so you can nail it in place. The opposite end will be either a butt joint (to fit against the wall or a door casing), a scarf joint (to join another length of cap molding), or an outside miter joint (to end at an outside corner of the wall). Repeat these last two steps until you've finished installing all the cap molding.

8 **MAKE THE SHOE FIT.** Install the shoe molding one piece at a time, working your way around the room as you did with board and cap pieces. All shoe joints can be mitered, and you can begin the installation at an inside corner. To install each piece, hold it firmly against the floor and drive the nail at a slight downward angle into the baseboard (not the floor).

9 **FINISH UP.** With cutting and nailing done, set all nail heads just below the wood surface, fill the holes with putty, sand surfaces smooth, and apply paint. While you're sanding the nail holes, use the sandpaper to slightly round over all outside miter joints.

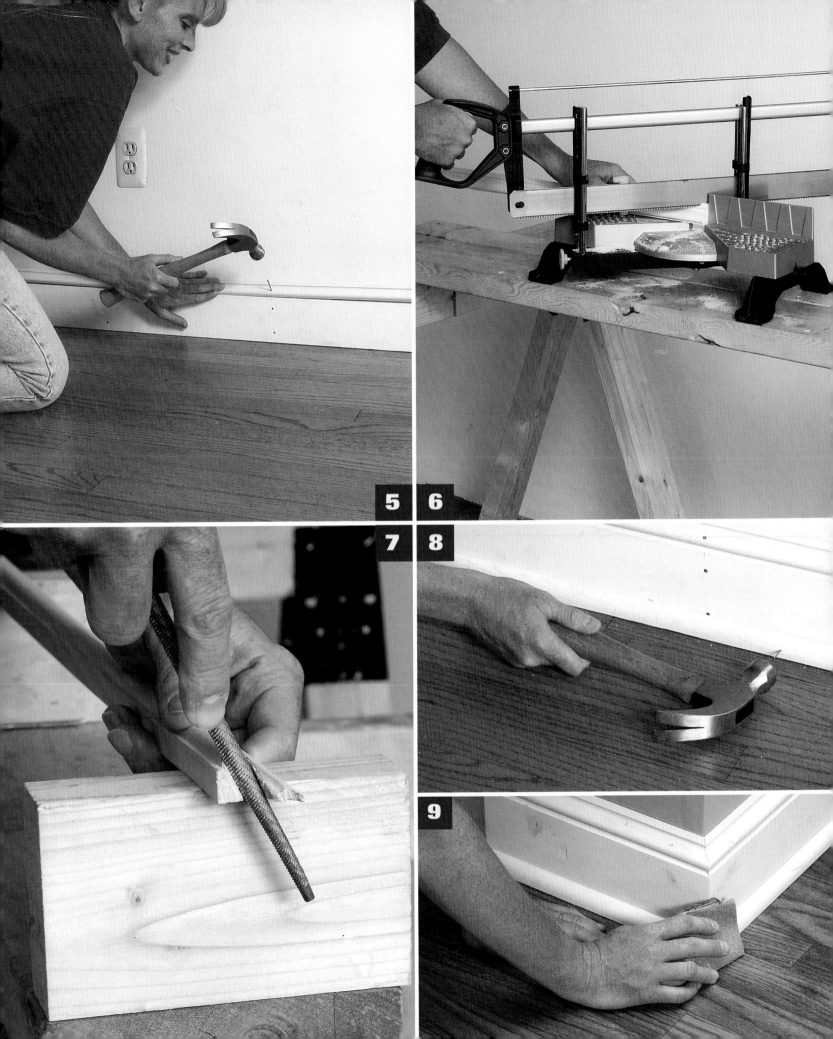

5 **6**

7 **8**

9

This built-in cabinet features an integral baseboard plinth that's beefy enough to offer a traditional, well-heeled appearance. Flat baseboard is trimmed with shoe molding and a base cap.

As the name suggests, baseboard can be thought of as the basis or beginning for any room's trim treatment. That's why you'll want to make sure the style and proportions of your baseboard relate well to other molding details, including built-in cabinetry. The design ideas shown here will help you get this dialog started.

A deep baseboard anchors this paneled wall, and provides plenty of space for installing receptacles. Make sure that door-jamb casing is deep enough so that the baseboard—and paneling in this case—can butt against it comfortably.

In this room, the baseboard was kept simple so the eye would naturally be drawn to the elaborate crown molding. Carpeted rooms should never use a shoe molding. Install baseboard before carpeting and butt the carpet to the baseboard.

It's not every day that you see baseboard and baseboard cap finished with contrasting colors, but why not? It's a cheery detail in this busy family home.

Post & Lintel

Even **BUTT JOINTS** can be beautiful. This easy trim treatment has plenty of variations you can try

BEFORE MACHINES BEGAN CHURNING out affordable moldings in the late 19th century, many homes were trimmed with flat boards. This simple casing scheme goes great with a "country" or "cottage-style" decorating plan.

Windows are trimmed at the top and sides exactly like passageway or door openings. The only difference is at the bottom, where side casings either land on a stool, as in this project, or meet another piece of casing. With colonial trim (see p. 24), a miter joint is used to achieve this "picture frame." Use butt joints for flat casings.

REMOVE THE OLD   INSTALL THE STOOL   INSTALL THE SIDES   INSTALL THE TOP

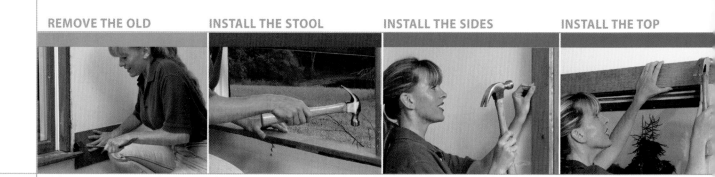

This cool tool is a stool—one of those toddlers use to reach the bathroom sink. One step up is all you need to work comfortably on the trim for most windows and doors—plus a stool is much less cumbersome than a ladder to move and work around. If you don't have a stool handy, an old milk crate will do the trick, too.

Before you install trim boards, give them a quick sanding to smooth out any rough spots or irregularities. If you plan to stain your casing, do this before installation, too. This way, you won't get stain on the walls.

Tools & Gear

Keep your basic tool kit handy because you'll need a hammer, tape measure, and nail set. You'll also need to gather up the gear described below.

CIRCULAR SAW. If you don't have a miter box for cutting your trim pieces to length, you can do the job with a circular saw and a finish-cutting blade.

DRILL & BIT. Predrilling nail holes helps you avoid splitting the wood, especially near the ends of boards. A corded or cordless drill will do the job, along with a tiny $1/16$-in.-dia. bit.

MITER BOX. A good miter box like the one used in this project comes with its own fine-tooth saw and costs about $40. Avoid cheaper wooden or plastic boxes that have slotted sides. If you want pro-level speed and precision, invest in a power miter saw.

COMBINATION SQUARE. This adjustable square is a versatile layout tool. For this project, you'll use it to lay out the reveals.

CAULKING GUN. You'll use this to dispense the caulk to seal the joint between wall and casing.

STEPLADDER OR STOOL. Unless you have unusually high openings or are short, you only need to get up about one step to trim a window. You can use any stepladder up to 6 feet, but a shorter one will be more convenient. Or grab a kid's stool such as described in COOL TOOL at left.

BRUSH, RAGS & RUBBER GLOVES. Clean, soft rags are the best way to stain wood. A good paintbrush is for applying varnish. The gloves are to keep stain off your hands.

What to Buy

1| CASING. The casing used here is 1x4 pine, which actually measures ³⁄₄ in. thick and 3¹⁄₂ in. wide. You'll need four pieces—the head casing, two side casing pieces, and the apron. Buy boards that are several inches longer than what your finished dimensions will be, and make sure each board is straight and flat.

2| STOOL. People often mistake the stool for the inside of the windowsill, but it is actually a separate piece. That's lucky for you, since you'll need to replace the stool if your new casing is wider than the old. If you're replacing the stool, take the old one with you to the lumberyard and get a new stool with the same cross section or profile.

1X4 PINE CASING ①
1X4 WINDOW STOOL ②
BOX OF 8D NAILS ③
④ **SANDPAPER**
CAULK ⑤

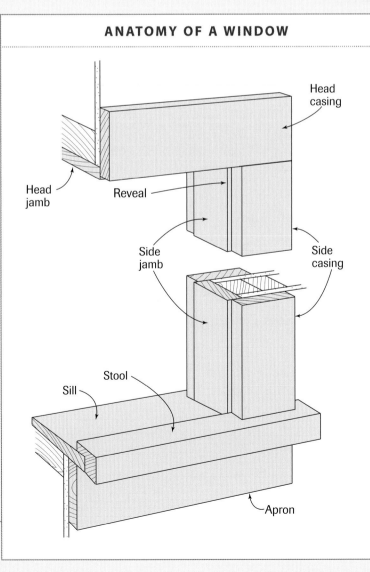

ANATOMY OF A WINDOW

Head casing

Head jamb

Reveal

Side jamb

Side casing

Stool

Sill

Apron

3| FINISH NAILS. You'll need 6d (2-in.) and 8d (2¹⁄₂-in.) finish nails to install all parts of this project.

4| SANDPAPER. Buy a couple of 9x11 sheets of 120-grit sandpaper, so you can sand putty patches smooth.

5| CAULK. Acrylic latex caulk is the type you want. You'll use it to fill any gaps caused by walls and ceilings that aren't flat or joinery that is less than perfect.

6| WOOD GLUE & PUTTY. Yellow wood glue will be used at joints. Putty is for filling nail holes.

7| STAIN & VARNISH. If you want to let the wood grain show, you can give your trim a clear varnish finish, or darken the wood with stain, followed by varnish for extra protection. Finish a scrap piece of wood first to make sure you've got the right tone and treatment.

Install the Stool

1 **REMOVE THE OLD APRON & STOOL.** Remove the old apron and casing, then carefully pry up the old stool, if there is one. Be careful not to damage the windowsill. On older windows, you may have to pry the window stop out of the way in order to remove the stool.

2 **CUT THE NEW STOOL.** The horns should extend past the casing by a distance equal to the thickness of the stool—usually ¾ in. or so. Cut the new stool to length. Center the old stool on the new stool, and use it as a template to lay out the horns. Cut the horns with a sabersaw or handsaw.

3 **INSTALL THE STOOL.** Round over the top edge of the stool a bit using some sandpaper. Fasten the stool to the sill with 8d finish nails spaced about 12 in. apart.

4 **LAY OUT THE REVEAL.** Casing typically is installed so as to leave about ⅛ in. of the jamb edge exposed. This exposed portion is called the reveal. To lay out the reveal, set a combination square to ⅛ in. Place a pencil in the notch in the end of the square's rule, and run the square around the side and head jambs.

1

2

3

4

When you place a piece of casing, you may discover it won't lie flat against the wall. See if the piece lies flat on the floor. If not, it's probably twisted and the best solution is to get another board. If it does lie flat, the problem is a bump in the wall or a protruding nail or screw. Run your hand down the wall or put a level against the wall to see where the problem is. Hammer or screw down any proud nails or screws.

Occasionally, the problem is so small you don't notice it until you've nailed the casing in place. In this case, since the casing is flat, a little sanding with a piece of sandpaper wrapped around a wood block will bring both sides of the joint into the same plane.

Install the Casing

5 **CUT THE SIDE CASING TO LENGTH.** Square-cut one end of the side casings, and cut them to rough length. If your miter saw won't cut your molding width, use a circular saw. Put the square-cut end of each side casing in place atop the stool, and mark where it crosses the reveal line on the head jamb. Cut the side casings to this length.

6 **INSTALL THE SIDE CASINGS.** Align the side casings to side jamb reveal lines, and fasten them with pairs of nails about every 2 ft. Use 6d finish nails for the jamb edge and 8d near the outside edges of the casing. Don't drive the nails all the way in. Instead, stop when the nail head is just above the wood surface.

7 **CUT THE HEAD CASING TO LENGTH.** Square-cut one end of the head casing, then put it atop the side casing. Align the square-cut end with the outside of a side casing, then mark the other end for cutting. Square-cut that end.

8 **INSTALL THE HEAD CASING.** Nail the head casing into place just as you did the side casing. The only difference is that the head casing gets an extra pair of nails on each end, just over the corner of the window opening. Check that all the joints are tight and in the right plane, then set the nails. Finally, round all the outside edges of the casing slightly using a piece of sandpaper.

9 **CUT & INSTALL THE APRON.** Measure across from the outside of one side casing to the outside of the other. Cut the apron to this length. Center it under the stool, and drive pairs of 8d nails into the wall and a few 4d nails down through the stool.

Off-the-shelf trim pieces can stack up to make elaborate door and window casings like these. Look for a thin stop molding between head and side casing and a thin cornice molding on top. Side jambs are pilaster-style casings, and aprons are embellished with bead moldings.

For an uber-Craftsman-style look, go for extra-wide head casing, stool, and apron, as you see here.

Create a wide variety of decorating schemes simply by changing the width or color of your post-and-lintel casings. Or embellish the casing with a band molding around the perimeter or a stop molding between the head casings and side casings. By using the stop molding along with a header cap, you can create a truly Craftsman-style motif. The Craftsman style is characterized by spare and careful use of architectural detail. The style emerged at the turn of the twentieth century in reaction to the highly ornate Victorian moldings that were so popular in the decades before.

Before you head to the lumberyard, make a list with the right lingo. For example, this Classically styled unpainted window has a bumper crop of trim, starting at the top with an ogee stop, a cornice molding, and a flat head casing atop a thinner flat casing. Jamb casings are flat but wide, and a roundover stool sits on an apron with a fancy edge.

Notice any recurring themes here? Take a look at the roundover header cap and the roundover stool on the window, which go nicely with a deep round-edged window seat and rounded stair treads.

Windows that crank out like the small awning window shown here often don't have stools. They look great with a simple "picture frame" post-and-lintel design. Just butt the side casings into the top casing and then butt a bottom casing against the bottom of the side pieces.

Wainscot

Thin TONGUE-&-GROOVE BOARDS make a durable, great-looking wall that's easy to install

ASOLID-WOOD WAINSCOT is a great upgrade for almost any wall. Apart from the beauty it adds, there are practical benefits, too. Wood stands up well to the hard knocks that come from chairs, kids, and wayward feet. No wonder wainscots are popular in entryways, mudrooms, breakfast nooks, and bathrooms.

The beadboard wainscot we're building here is a traditional treatment that's easy to do. If the wall surface is smooth and flat, you can install the ⅜-in.-thick beadboard with panel adhesive. There's very little nailing to do until we get to the baseboard and cap parts of the project. You've probably got your wainscot room picked out already, so get your tape measure out and let's get started.

LAY IT OUT   FIT THE INSIDE CORNERS   THEN THE OUTSIDE CORNERS   BASEBOARD & CAP

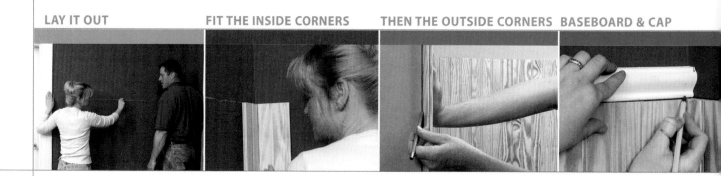

⊙ DO IT RIGHT

There's no rule about how high to make a wainscot as long as you don't divide the wall in half, which can look awkward. The room shown in this project has 9-ft. walls, and the wainscot is 5 ft. high for a farmhouse look.

✦ DO IT NOW

You don't need to know stud locations to install the beadboard, but you do for the cap molding. An easy way to confirm stud locations is to drive a finish nail through the drywall in the spot where you think a stud may be. It's easy to tell when you hit a stud and when you don't. Do your test-nailing below the top edge of the wainscot, and make a pencil mark where you find each stud.

Tools & Gear

Keep your basic tool kit handy because you'll need a hammer, tape measure, and nail set.

DRILL & BIT. Predrilling your nail holes will help to avoid splitting the wood. A cordless drill and $\frac{1}{16}$-in. bit will do the job.

CHOPSAW OR MITER BOX. Either of these tools will handle the precise crosscuts and miters you need to make when installing the cap, baseboard, base cap, and shoe trim. A chopsaw is the faster way to go.

CIRCULAR SAW. Put a finish-cutting blade in your saw; you'll need it for cutting beadboard and baseboard pieces.

BLOCK PLANE. This small handplane will help you fine-tune the fit of outside corners.

ROUND FILE. You'll need a "rat-tail" file to fine-tune the cope joints in the cap moldings.

FOUR-FOOT LEVEL. You'll need a 4-ft. level to scribe level lines for the top of the wainscot.

CHALKLINE. This is to extend the level lines you make with the 4-ft. level.

CAULKING GUN. You'll use this to dispense construction adhesive and caulk.

COPING SAW. This small saw has a thin blade held in a C-shaped frame. You'll need it to cope the chair rail and (if you don't have a jigsaw) for making the cutouts for electrical switch and outlet boxes.

What to Buy

1 | BEADBOARD. $^3/_8$-in.-thick tongue-and-groove beadboard (also called beaded board) used in this project is available in different widths; $3^1/_8$ in. and $5^1/_4$ in. are the most common. For this project, we used $3^1/_8$-in.-wide boards. At home centers, beadboard paneling comes packed in bundles of boards that are 4 ft. or 8 ft. long. At lumberyards, it's sold in 2-ft. length increments. To calculate how much to buy, add up the length of your walls and subtract the window and door widths. Divide the result by the width of your beaded boards. For example, if you have 480 inches of wall length, 480 divided by 3 means you'll need about 160 boards that are $3^1/_8$ in. wide, or 92 boards in $5^1/_4$-in. width.

2 | WAINSCOT CAP. This molding fits over the top of the beadboard. Several styles are available—just make sure you get a cap molding designed to fit over $^3/_8$-in.-thick boards.

3 | BASEBOARD, BASE CAP & SHOE. To go with the wide casings and traditional moldings in this old house, the bottom of the wainscot is covered with a 1x8 baseboard along with base cap and shoe. Your plan might call for a different baseboard height with or without the shoe and/or cap. Or you might choose a molded, one-piece baseboard.

4 | FINISH NAILS. You'll need 4d ($1^1/_2$-in.) finish nails to install the base cap, 8d ($2^1/_2$-in.) nails for the baseboard, and 1-in. brads for the base shoe.

5 | SANDPAPER. Use 120-grit sandpaper to sand putty patches for molding that will be painted.

6 | CONSTRUCTION ADHESIVE. Several cartridges should give you enough for an average-sized room.

7 | YELLOW GLUE. Have this wood glue on hand for gluing miters and molding together.

8 | CAULK & PUTTY. Paintable latex acrylic caulk is the type you want. You'll use it to fill gaps and cover seams. The putty is for filling nail holes.

9 | PRIMER & PAINT. If you plan to paint your molding, get primer recommended for use on bare wood. Also get some acrylic semigloss paint for interior trim.

PUTTING IT ALL TOGETHER

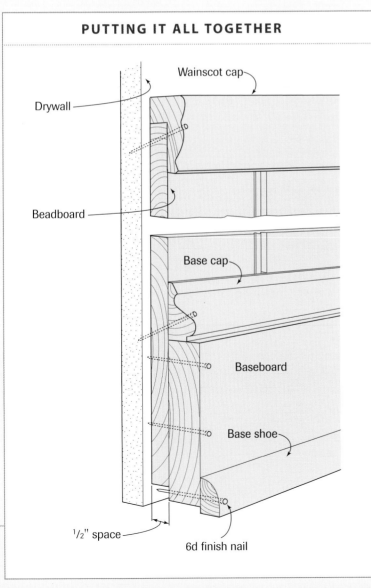

Wainscot cap

Drywall

Beadboard

Base cap

Baseboard

Base shoe

$^1/_2$" space

6d finish nail

Now that lower-priced models are available, you might consider buying a laser level. This layout tool shoots a thin beam of light across the room, making it easy to quickly get level marks in numerous spots. It's quick, accurate, and easy to carry in a toolbox. Prices begin around $65.

Since most of your boards will need to be cut to the same length, you can save time by cutting several boards at once with a circular saw. You can place several boards across some sawhorses, mark the cut line, and make the cut.

Install the First Walls

1 **LAY OUT THE TOP OF THE WAINSCOT.** Mark the height of the wainscot in one corner of the room, then use your level to draw a level line about 4 ft. long. Have a helper hold a chalkline at the other corner, exactly covering the line. Snap the line and check that it is level. Mark level lines on all walls.

2 **CUT BOARDS TO LENGTH.** Keep in mind that the cap will overlap the tops of the boards, and the baseboard will cover bottom board edges. There's no need to make your cuts supersmooth or to land exactly on the layout line.

3 **BEGIN AT A CORNER.** Start at the room's most visible inside corner. Apply construction adhesive to the back of a board, then press the board in place, with the tongue butted into the corner. Install the other corner piece, this time with the groove butting into the corner, covering the tongue.

Next, work your way out from the corner, installing one board after another. Make sure to fit the tongue-and-groove joints together. Stop when you get two boards away from a doorway or another inside corner.

4 **FIT THE LAST INSIDE CORNER PIECE.** At runs that end at doorways or inside corners, put the second-to-last board into place without adhesive. Measure the space where the final board has to fit, then measure at the top and bottom of the wainscot, in case the cut needs to taper slightly.

Transfer your measurements to the last board, and cut along the line with a jigsaw or a circular saw. Test-fit the last two boards. If necessary, fine-tune the fit by planing the edge of the last board with a block plane.

⊙ **DO IT RIGHT**

When you encounter an outlet box, mark where you have to notch your boards and cut the notches with a jigsaw or coping saw. You'll also need to install ³/₈-in. box extenders. Ask for these at your home center or hardware store. To install an extender, turn the power off, remove the cover plate, and unscrew the receptacle or switch from the box. Without disconnecting the wires, install the extender and reattach the receptacle or switch.

Corners, Caps & Baseboards

5 **INSTALL THE LAST TWO INSIDE CORNER PIECES.** Spread adhesive on the last two pieces, and press them into place. Don't worry if there's a small gap between the molding and the corner; you'll cover it with caulk later.

6 **MARK FOR AN OUTSIDE CORNER.** When you get to a piece that will have to be cut to meet an outside corner, put it in place and mark the cut along its back. Use a jigsaw or circular saw to make the cut, taking care to stay on the "waste" side of the line. Then

smooth the cut with a block plane. Plane up to the line, but don't plane the line away. You want the piece to extend just slightly past the corner to ensure a tight joint. Install the piece when you're done.

7 **INSTALL THE SECOND OUTSIDE CORNER PIECE.** Mark the overlapping corner piece by holding it in place, as you did in step 6, then cut it and install it. You can plane for the final fit after the piece is in place. To close up the corner joint, use some yellow glue. If necessary, you can drive a few ¾-in. brads, too. Take a break when you get all your boards on the wall. Great job so far.

8 **INSTALL THE BASEBOARD & CAP, THEN FINISH UP.** Follow the steps on pp. 48–51 to install the baseboard, base cap, and shoe moldings. The cap molding that tops off the wainscot is also installed with cope joints at inside corners and miter joints at outside corners. The only

difference is that you need to trim off the notch to butt a cap piece against the wall. Mark the cut, then make it with a coping saw. Now it's time to call in the finishing crew. Caulk the seams, fill the nail holes, sand, and paint.

Above: This painted beadboard makes a durable finished wall in an informal dining area.

Above right: Don't think that a small space can't take wainscot. This bathroom tucked under the roof actually looks bigger paneled with an all-white wainscot and fixtures. Make sure your baseboard has enough height to balance the look of wainscot, as it does here.

Beadboard adds durability and visual interest just about anywhere in your home. In addition to being used for wainscot paneling, beadboard is the traditional material for porch ceilings, for example.

Today, the beadboard look doesn't necessarily mean installing individual tongue-and-groove strips. As an alternative, you can use 4-ft. by 8-ft. sheets of beaded plywood.

Here's another take on how to handle the horizontal trim that caps a wainscot. Around a tub—and on the ceiling, where humidity is high—painted beadboard provides a tougher surface than painted drywall, and it adds a traditional flair.

This sunroom shows how versatile beaded tongue-and-groove boards can be. They are used floor to ceiling, as well as on the ceiling itself. The boards also make a shoe-resistant surface on a bench fitted with custom-made cushions.

Picture-Frame Wainscot

If you can assemble frames of **MITERED MOLDING**, you've got a dramatic way to wake up a flat wall

AS SOON AS PLASTER BEGAN replacing wooden walls in the mid-18th century, architects started looking for ways to embellish these smooth, flat surfaces. The solution in many homes was the pleasingly regular look created with rectangles of narrow molding.

Today the wall surface is drywall, not plaster. But the problem and solution are the same. This wainscot combines a horizontal chair-rail molding with rectangular "picture frames" made with miter joints. You'll find plenty of ways to be creative here, from choosing your own molding profiles to selecting frame size and spacing and deciding on your finishing strategy.

CUT THE COPE   CUT THE FRAME   PUT IT TOGETHER   FINISH UP

▶ DO IT RIGHT

The key to making frames quickly and accurately is to set up a stop block for your miter box. The block enables you to duplicate parts without any measuring. Start by cutting a "master" piece to the length you want, mitered on both ends. With the piece against the fence, put one end against the blade and use the other end to position the stop block. Clamp the block in place. (For more on setting up a miter saw, see p. 20.) You'll need to reposition the block to cut a different length.

❖ COOL TOOL

Do yourself a favor: Rent or borrow a power finish nailer for this job. Pro trim carpenters swear by these tools, and you'll soon understand why. In addition to speeding the work, a power nailer allows you to hold the part with one hand while you trigger the nailer with the other. The part doesn't shift around or split when you nail it. You don't even need to set the nail head below the wood surface; the nailer does this for you. Power nailers are safe and easy to use if you follow the manufacturer's directions.

Tools & Gear

Keep your basic tool kit handy, and round up the gear described below. This project will go a lot faster if you've got a couple of key power tools.

CHOPSAW. Although you can complete this project by making miter cuts by hand with a regular miter box, the job will go much faster if you use a motorized miter saw. Basic models sell for less than $100, but you can also rent or borrow this tool.

POWER NAILER. A finish nailer is what you want. Whether you borrow, rent, or buy your nailer, you'll appreciate the speed and precision the tool helps you to achieve (see COOL TOOL at left).

FOUR-FOOT LEVEL. You'll need a 4-ft. level to lay out the frame positions on the wall and establish a level line for installing the chair-rail molding.

CHALKLINE. By "snapping" chalklines, you'll be able to extend level layout lines all around the room.

CAULKING GUN. You'll use this to dispense construction adhesive and caulk.

CIRCULAR SAW. You'll need one to make the frame-assembly jig.

COPING SAW. This small saw is what you need to make the cope cuts in the chair-rail molding. Blades can break easily, so have some spares on hand.

ROUND FILE. With a round "rat-tail" file, you can fine-tune any cope joint.

SPRING CLAMPS. You'll need two medium-sized spring clamps to assemble the frames.

What to Buy

1| FRAME MOLDING. You can make the picture frames from any narrow molding you like. Here we used a 1¼-in.-wide base cap. You'll need to sketch out your wainscot design to calculate how much molding to buy (see "Planning the Project" below).

2| CHAIR-RAIL MOLDING. This molding runs horizontally around the room, defining the top of the wainscot. Choose a chair-rail profile you like, and buy enough to go around the room, with about 10% extra length added in case you have to recut a joint or two.

3| PLYWOOD. To make the base of the frame-assembly jig, you'll need a rectangular piece of ¾-in. plywood about 14 in. wide and 24 in. long.

4| SOLID WOOD. Make the jig's guide boards from 1x4 that's about 24 in. long.

5| FINISH NAILS. You'll need 1½-in. nails to pin the moldings to the drywall until the adhesive grabs. If you use a power nailer, be sure to get nails designed to work in your nail gun.

6| CAULK. A cartridge of painter's latex caulk is what you need for this job.

7| CONSTRUCTION ADHESIVE. Buy a cartridge for your caulking gun; it's for adhering the moldings to the wall.

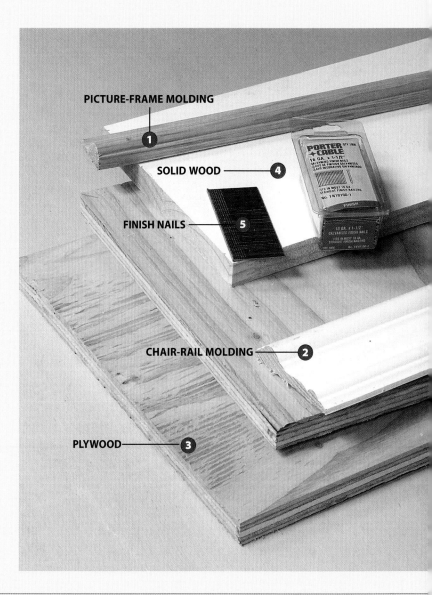

PICTURE-FRAME MOLDING ①

SOLID WOOD ④

FINISH NAILS ⑤

CHAIR-RAIL MOLDING ②

PLYWOOD ③

PLANNING THE PROJECT

After choosing the molding for your picture frames, the next design decision involves the size of your frames and the spacing between them. Make a scale drawing of the walls you'll be transforming. Include locations of windows, doorways, existing baseboard molding, and electrical outlets. Draw in the chair rail first; it's typically located about 34 in. from the floor. The chair-rail molding can butt against window side casings that interrupt its run. Beneath a window, plan a square or rectangular frame spaced a symmetrical distance away from adjacent frames. In this project, we used vertically oriented frames, with 2½-in. spaces at top, bottom, and sides. Based on your sketch, make a cut list that includes the lengths of frame pieces and chair-rail molding.

DO IT RIGHT

If your coping saw blade starts to twist while going around a tight corner, back the blade out of the cut and saw straight in from the outside edge to remove some waste. This will make room for the saw to maneuver without twisting the blade.

Install the Chair Rail

1 **"SNAP" THE CHAIR-RAIL LINE & LOCATE STUDS.** In a corner, measure up to the height you've selected for the chair rail. Use a 4-ft. level to draw a level line at that point. Have a helper stretch a chalkline to the opposite corner, keeping the line on the level. Pull the line away from the wall and "snap" it against the wall to mark where the chair rail will go. Mark level lines on all walls, and use a stud finder to mark stud locations along the chair-rail line.

2 **INSTALL THE FIRST RAIL.** Start with the most visible wall in the room—it's usually the one opposite the door. Cut both ends of a piece of chair rail at 90 degrees to fit. Using your caulking gun, apply construction adhesive on the back of the molding, then press the molding in place on the wall. Drive a 6d finish nail at each stud location. To close gaps, you can drive 4d finish nails between studs.

3 **EXPOSE THE COPE PROFILE.** The remaining chair-rail pieces will be coped on one end and butted on the other. (If you have an outside corner in the room, cut miter joints as shown in step 5.) The first step in cutting a cope is to make a 45-degree cut as if you were making an inside miter joint. Make these angled cuts using a chopsaw.

4 **CUT & TUNE THE COPE.** Cut out the 45-degree profile with your coping saw, cutting away any wood that prevents the joint from fitting tightly against the butted piece. Test-fit and fine-tune the joint

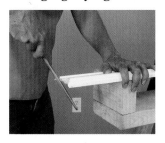

using a round file. When the cope fits, hold it in place, then mark the opposite end to be cut. Install each piece of chair rail as you cut and file it to fit, using construction adhesive and finish nails as in step 2.

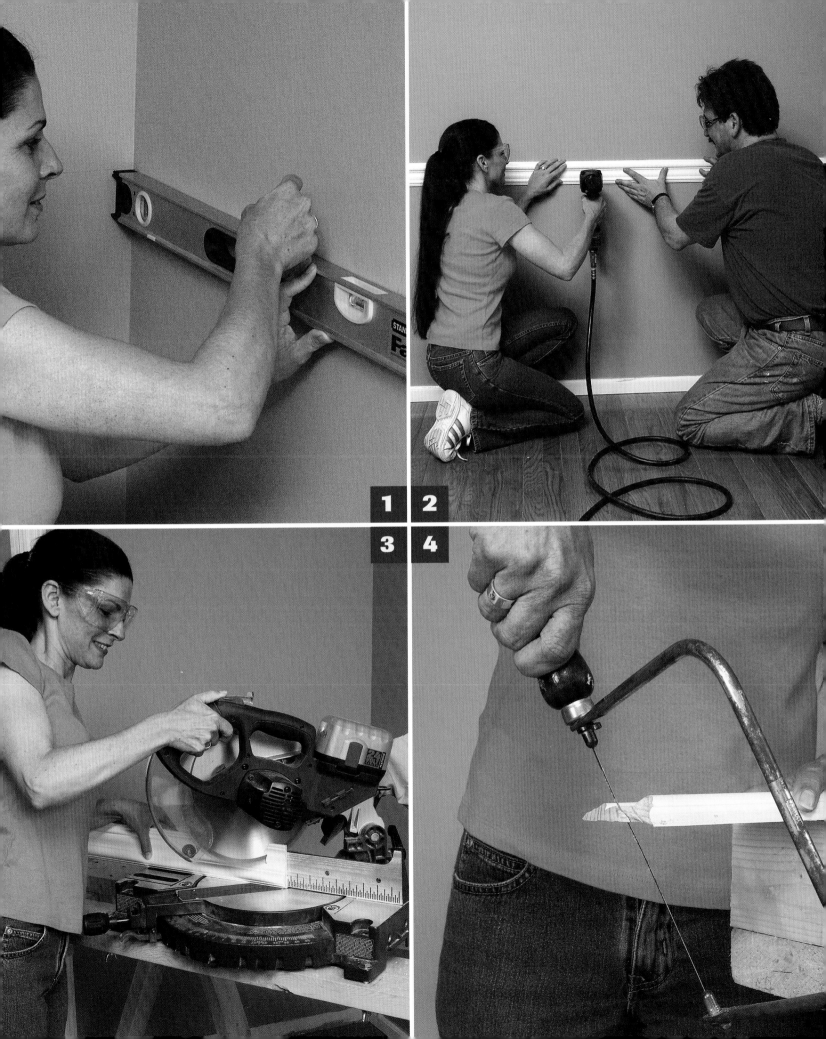

1

2

3

4

Ready the Frames

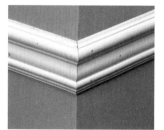

5 **MITER OUTSIDE CORNERS.** To install chair-rail molding around an outside corner, mark each piece at the corner, then cut an outside miter joint using a chopsaw. Glue the miter joint when you install both pieces of chair rail.

6 **CUT THE FRAME PIECES.** Since frames will be assembled from sets of same-sized pieces, now is the time to measure and cut one piece of each size you'll need to duplicate. Based on your cutting list (see "Planning the Project" on p. 77), measure and cut your master pieces. Use each master piece to position a stop block on your chopsaw workstation, and cut all same-sized pieces by butting the molding against the stop block. Cut all duplicate pieces this way.

7 **MARK FRAME LOCATIONS.** In the wainscot shown here, the tops of the frames are 2½ in. from the bottom of the chair rail, though your spacing may be different. Cut a piece of wood as a spacer, and run it along the bottom of the chair rail to guide a pencil line for the top of the frames. Then lay out the top corner of each frame along the line.

8 **MAKE AN ASSEMBLY JIG.** You'll drive yourself nuts if you try to assemble the frames on the wall piece by piece. Instead, assemble them "on the flat," using a simple picture-frame jig. Make the jig's base from a rectangular piece of ¾-in. plywood. Glue and nail two straight guide boards to the base, about 1½ in. from the plywood edge. Each guide board can be about ¾ in. thick and 1 in. wide. Make sure the guide boards form a square corner.

Nail 'em Up

9 **ASSEMBLE YOUR FRAMES.** Secure the jig to a work surface so it won't slide around. Spread some glue on the miter joints for two frame pieces, then clamp them in the jig so the miter joint fits tightly. Drive a 1½-in. finish nail into the joint from both sides, then wipe off excess glue with a damp cloth. Assemble all your frames using the jig.

10 **INSTALL THE FRAMES.** Apply small dabs of construction adhesive every few inches along the back of each frame. Press the frame onto the wall, aligning the frame with the layout marks you made in step 7. Anchor the frame in place with 1½-in. nails. Don't worry if you're not driving these nails into studs; the nails are just to hold the frames in place while the adhesive sets.

11 **NAIL THE SIDES & BOTTOMS.** To make sure your frames are level and aligned with each other, use a level in combination with spacer blocks. Finish nailing all frames in place, and wipe off any construction adhesive that squeezes out onto the wall.

12 **FINISH THE JOB.** Your wall already looks great, and you haven't even painted it yet. Caulk the seams where frames meet the wall, taking care to smooth your caulk joints with a damp rag. Fill all nail holes with putty and sand the putty smooth when it dries. Paint your wainscot and frames before painting the walls, using an acrylic semigloss trim paint.

9

10

11

12

Here's your chance to really get the creative juices flowing. Light walls with dark picture frames and dark walls with light frames are two choices that come immediately to mind. But how about painting the walls and frames the same color—or nearly the same color? This lets the molding shape do the job of adding visual interest. Or add another element to the frames—like the second wrap of picture frame that enhances the dining room at left. Don't hesitate to apply molding frames over wallpaper, as in the bedroom below.

Top: Two wraps of molding applied to pale green walls create elegant full-length picture frames. The inner frame is 1^9/$_{32}$-in.-wide decorative molding, while the outer frame is 1^{15}/$_{16}$-in.-wide chair-rail molding.

Bottom: Subtly painted molding frames add detail to wainscot without stealing the spotlight from the corner cupboard.

Picture-rail trim and chair-rail molding can be applied directly to drywall, but for a beefier look to a wainscot, add wood paneling or even a thin, additional layer of drywall before attaching trim. Consider relocating receptacles to the baseboard for a cleaner look.

Elegance comes easily when you apply picture-frame wainscot and chair rail over wallpaper, as in this bedroom.

Look closely to see that wainscot trim and paneling are painted the same color—just a tad lighter than the wall color above. It's a subtle touch that's appropriate in an elegant dining room where the emphasis is on wood with natural finishes. Here's a painter's secret: Brush paint—don't roll or spray—on the entire wainscot to make drywall look like wood paneling.

Contemporary Cornice

Transform the top of your wall with a simple CROWN MOLDING

THE DIFFERENCE BETWEEN "CORNICE" AND "CROWN" is difficult to explain. But whatever terminology you use, this trim treatment for the top of a room is almost always a good idea. Installing a crown or cornice molding is an excellent way to create a graceful transition where walls and ceilings meet.

While a decorative cornice can be made up of several different moldings, it's better to go with a smaller and simpler molding if your ceilings are around 8 ft. high. The techniques shown here will work with any of the many crown molding profiles you'll find at home centers and lumberyards. Find a profile you like, and get started.

| LAY IT OUT | SCARFS FIRST | COPING WELL | OUTSIDE MITERS |

▶ **DO IT RIGHT**

"Upside down and backwards" is the way many trim carpenters describe their approach to cutting crown molding. That's because the molding is oriented this way on your chopsaw or miter box. Imagine that the flat base of the saw is the ceiling and the vertical back fence of the saw is the wall, and place your molding accordingly.

✳ **DO IT FAST**

Although crown molding can be tricky to transport, it's smart to buy it in long lengths, so you don't have to join pieces together in the middle of a wall. Eliminating midwall joints saves time and creates a better finished appearance.

Tools & Gear

Your basic tool kit will come in handy for this project, and you'll need some extra gear as well. Here's what it takes, tool-wise, to complete this trim transformation.

DRILL & BIT. It's always a good idea to predrill nail holes near the ends of molding pieces to prevent the pieces from splitting. A cordless drill with a $\frac{1}{16}$-in. bit will do the trick.

CHOPSAW. You can make cornice cuts by hand, using a standard miter box. But a power miter saw gets the job done faster. Basic chopsaws like the one used on this project are available for less than $100. You can also rent or borrow one; just make sure it has a finish-cutting blade.

COPING SAW. This tool has a thin blade held in a C-shaped frame. It's what you need to cut the tight curves for the cope joints in this project. Blades break easily, so have some spares on hand.

CAULKING GUN. You'll use this to dispense the caulk to fill gaps in joints and between the molding and the wall and ceiling.

FILES. With a small flat file and a round "rat-tail" file, you can fine-tune any cope joint.

STEPLADDERS. It's time to pay your neighbor a visit. To put up long runs of molding, you'll need a pair of 6-ft. stepladders.

TRIM BRUSH. Your new trim deserves a nice finish. Apply it with a high-quality trim brush that's $1\frac{1}{2}$ in. to 2 in. wide. If you're using oil-based finish, make sure to use a natural-bristle brush or a synthetic brush recommended for use with oil or alkyd finishes.

COOL TOOL

Stop blocks make your chopsaw work more accurately by helping to keep pieces of molding positioned correctly as you cut them. You can make stop blocks from short, straight lengths of wood, and anchor them in place with screws or clamps. Trick your brain into thinking that the back fence on your saw is the wall, and the horizontal base of the saw is the ceiling. Position a pair of stop blocks (one on either side of the blade) to hold the molding in this upside-down orientation. As shown in the photo at right, the installation angle of the molding will determine the proper location for each stop block.

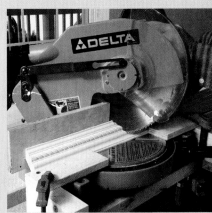

What to Buy

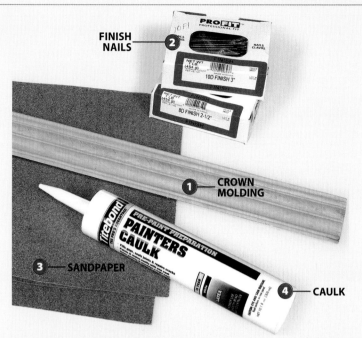

FINISH NAILS

CROWN MOLDING

SANDPAPER

CAULK

1 | CROWN MOLDING. Many sizes and styles of this molding are available. A smaller profile (like the one used in this project) is a good idea in any room with an 8-ft. or lower ceiling. The length of the pieces you purchase depends on the dimensions of your room and where you want joints to fall. (See "Planning Your Joints" below). Buy at least 15% more than the finished installation demands.

2 | FINISH NAILS. To install this molding, we used 8d (2½-in.) and 10d (3-in.) finish nails. For a thinner crown molding, go with 4d and 6d finish nails.

3 | SANDPAPER. Use 120-grit sandpaper to sand putty patches and smooth outside corners.

4 | CAULK. Latex painter's caulk is the type you need. You'll use it to fill any gaps caused by walls and ceilings that aren't flat or joinery that is less than perfect.

5 | WOOD GLUE & PUTTY. Yellow wood glue will be used at joints. Putty is for filling nail holes.

6 | PRIMER & PAINT. If you plan to paint your molding, use a good-quality primer under two coats of semigloss trim paint.

Planning Your Joints

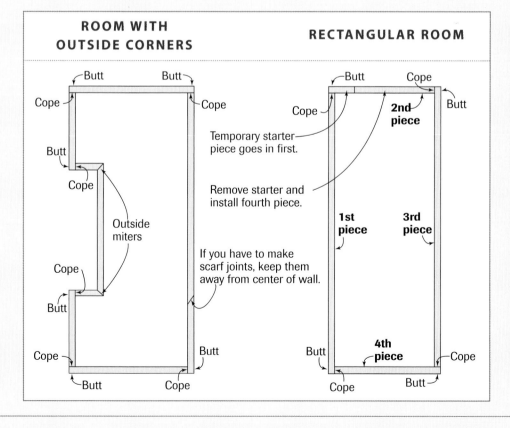

ROOM WITH OUTSIDE CORNERS

RECTANGULAR ROOM

Butt — Butt

Cope — Cope

Butt — Cope

Cope — Butt

Temporary starter piece goes in first.

2nd piece

Butt

Cope

Remove starter and install fourth piece.

Outside miters

1st piece — **3rd piece**

Cope

If you have to make scarf joints, keep them away from center of wall.

Butt

Cope — Butt

4th piece

Butt — Cope

Butt — Cope

Cope — Butt

Draw a plan view of the room where your cornice will be installed, then spend a few minutes figuring out what joints will be used where. Every inside corner will have one piece of molding that simply extends to butt against the wall and a joining piece that must be coped to fit against it. Avoid having a single piece that must be coped at both ends. Instead, plan your joints so that one end can be coped and the other can butt against the wall or join another piece of molding with a scarf joint (see step 10 on p. 94). If your room includes outside corners, that's no problem. These outside miters are easy to mark and cut.

Lay It Out

1 **SCRIBE A GUIDELINE.** Make a scribe block as described in DO IT FAST at left, then hold the block against the ceiling as you scribe a line on the wall for the bottom of the molding.

2 **MARK STUDS & CEILING JOISTS.** Using a stud finder, locate the first stud out from the corner. Confirm the location by driving a finish nail into the wall above your scribe line. When you hit a stud, hook a tape measure on the nail, and look for the studs at 16-in. intervals. Mark all stud locations on your scribe line. Do the same for ceiling joists, but don't worry if you can't locate them; we'll solve that problem in step 4.

3 **CUT SCARF JOINTS.** If a wall requires a scarf joint because it is too long for one piece of molding, start with the piece that will be butted into the corner. Cut the butt end square, then mark your scarf-joint cut directly over a stud. Make the scarf cut on a chopsaw; it's the same 45-degree cut you'd make for an inside miter joint. Repeat this step along other walls where a butt-and-scarf piece is required.

4 **INSTALL THE FIRST PIECE.** With a helper holding up one end of the molding, install the first piece by driving an 8d finish nail at every stud and ceiling joist location. Make sure the bottom edge of the molding stays on your scribe line. If no ceiling joists cross the wall, you can drive a second finish nail above your first nails, but there's no need to do this if the top of the molding is against the ceiling.

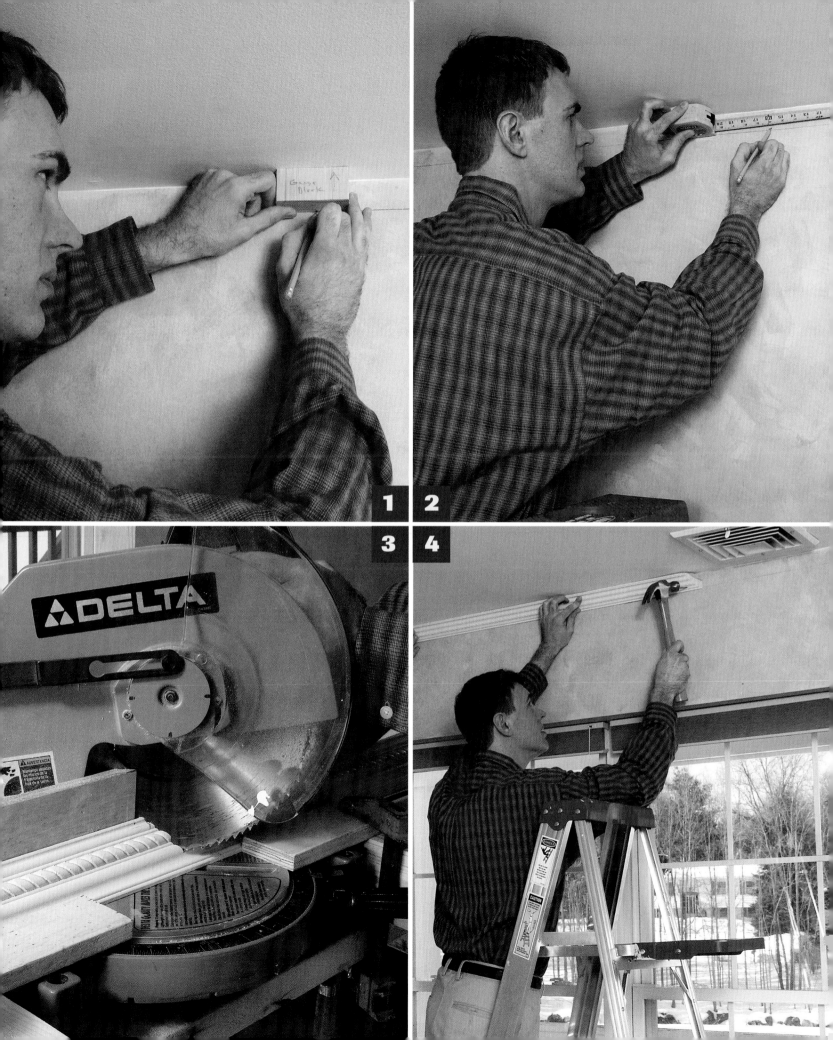

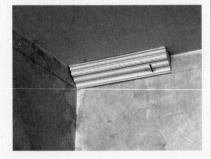
Cut the Copes

5 **EXPOSE THE COPE PROFILE.** In the room shown here, the first cope joint will be on the right-hand end of the molding piece. Turn the piece upside down so that the edge that will be at the ceiling is on the saw base, and place it to the right of the miter-saw blade. Make the cut with the blade at 45 degrees to your right. This reveals the profile you will cope.

6 **CUT THE FIRST COPE.** Use your coping saw to cut along the profile, angling the saw toward the back of the molding. Don't make sharp turns that will twist the blade. Instead, back out of the cut and then cut in from the edge to remove a chunk of the inside miter.

7 **FINE-TUNE THE COPE.** Test-fit the cope against a piece of scrap, and fine-tune it with a flat file and/or a round file. If there are gaps, it's probably not an inaccuracy in the way you cut the profile. Usually you just need to file away a little more material from the back of the molding.

8 **CUT COPED PIECES TO LENGTH.** Measuring from the bottom of the cope joint—where the molding is longest—mark the other end for a butt or scarf cut. For a butt-cut full-length piece, make the 90-degree cut so that the pencil line is still visible when you are done, then test-fit the piece. Ideally, the piece should bow out very slightly, so that you need to press on it lightly to hold it flat against the wall.

No helper to hold one end of the tape while you stretch it across the top of the wall to take a measurement? Tack a finish nail halfway in as close to the corner as you can. Hook the end of the tape over the nail, then bend the nail toward the corner to tightly capture the tape's hook while you pull the tape to the other wall.

WHAT CAN GO WRONG

Wall and ceiling surfaces aren't always as flat as they look. Don't be upset if you see some gaps between the edges of the molding and the wall and ceiling. It's easy to seal these gaps with caulk, and once you do, nobody but you will know they were ever there.

Miter Outside Corners

9 **INSTALL COPED PIECES.** Transfer nailing locations to the molding, then put glue on the coped end. While a helper holds the coped joint tight, drive installation nails near the middle of the piece, then work your way toward the ends. If the room has no outside corners, keep installing the remaining pieces in the same manner.

10 **COMPLETE SCARF JOINTS.** If you need to complete a scarf joint, make the cope on the other end as in steps 6–8, but cut an outside miter to overlap the inside miter on the first scarfed piece you installed. Glue the scarf joint as well as the coped joint when you install  the piece, and drive one or two finish nails through the scarf joint (after predrilling nail holes) to pull the joint together. Repeat wherever you have more scarf joints. If your room has no outside corners, go to the last part of step 12.

11 **MARK & CUT OUTSIDE CORNER PIECES.** If you need to turn an outside corner with your cornice, cut one side of the joint at a time. With the opposite end of the molding already cut to fit, let the molding run long, beyond the outside corner, and mark where the miter cut needs to be made. On your chopsaw, align the blade to the waste side of your mark, and make the 45-degree miter cut. Tack this first outside miter piece in place, then mark and cut the joining piece.

12 **COMPLETE OUTSIDE MITERS, THEN FILL, SAND & FINISH.** Spread glue on mating miter pieces before nailing them in place. Next, set all nails, fill the holes with putty, and caulk the seams between molding edges and wall and ceiling surfaces. Fill gaps in miter and cope joints with caulk, and wipe them smooth with a damp rag. When the caulk has dried, sand the molding smooth, then apply primer and finish coats of paint.

9 **10**

11 **12**

Just because it's called baseboard doesn't mean you have to use it that way. Here two pieces of common single-piece baseboard fit together at the ceiling and wall junction. Top them with an equally common crown molding and you have an uncommon cornice treatment in a hurry.

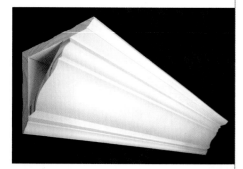

A beadboard ceiling and crown molding create an elegant effect over an arched entryway.

Crown molding isn't just relegated to the top of a wall. This molding not only trims the top of framed openings but cuts across extra tall walls to add flair and keep the scale of the rooms more intimate.

A graceful transition between walls and ceiling, crown molding makes any room feel more comfortable. It also adds an air of craftsmanship. If embellishments are what you're after, think about doing a "built-up" profile. The example shown above left, using two pieces of baseboard molding under the crown, is an easy way to amplify the impact of stock crown molding. Just attach the baseboard pieces with construction adhesive and a few nails or screws to hold the pieces up while the adhesive grabs. Then nail the crown to the continuous wood surfaces.

There's a lot of molding action going on in this room, but subtle color differences make the room look warm and inviting instead of overly busy. The darker taupe wainscot panels anchor the room while the lighter toned taupe-and-white speckled walls create an airy transition between white moldings, including the understated 5½-in.-wide dentil crown molding.

Left: Feel free to break the mold when it comes to where trim goes and how it is finished. In this kitchen, white-painted crown molding helps reinforce the style set by the stained crown molding that tops the cherry cabinetry.

A tall room just isn't complete without crown molding, especially if the look is traditional. Don't skimp on size—this deep crown molding fits the scale of the room. Paint molding white like the ceiling to make the room look bigger and brighter.

Crowning Touch

This intricate **CORNICE MOLDING** looks like plaster, but it's made from lightweight foam & can simply be glued in place

AN INTRICATELY DETAILED CORNICE can be the perfect topper for a room with a noble purpose, a high ceiling, or both. And if you take advantage of the lightweight foam moldings available today, this trim treatment can be far easier to accomplish than the finished results suggest. The urethane foam used in this type of molding makes the material much lighter than wood, so it's easier to handle. Foam molding won't split, crack, or warp, either, and it comes with a factory-applied coat of primer. A number of different profiles are available, so you can find something that suits your style. Once you do, plan to have a helper for this project because you'll need someone to hold up the other end.

| CUT THE FIRST MITERS | STICKY STUFF | NAIL IT UP | CAULK & FINISH |

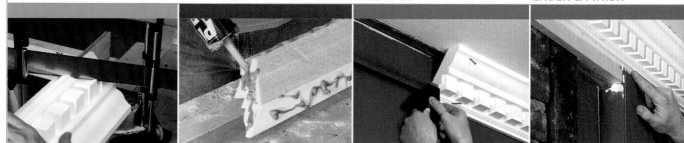

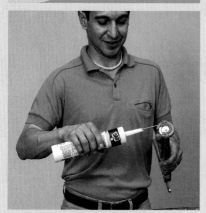

If you need to buy a caulking gun, avoid the cheapest models. As with other tools, a little extra money can buy you a lot of extra value. A top-notch gun will have a larger handle to give you some extra leverage for squeezing the caulk out. Two other features to look for: A built-in rod you can use to pierce the seal on a caulk canister and a built-in snip for cutting the plastic tip.

Tools & Gear

Keep your basic tool kit handy because you'll need a hammer, nail set, and tape measure for this project.

MITER BOX. To make smooth, accurate cuts in the crown molding, you'll need a miter box that comes with its own fine-tooth saw. To cut wide moldings like the one used in this project, you may need to attach a tall plywood auxiliary fence to your miter box. Check out COOL TOOL on the facing page.

CAULKING GUN. You'll need one to dispense the adhesive that bonds the molding to the wall and ceiling.

PUTTY KNIFE. Get a putty knife with a small (1-in.-wide) and flexible blade; you'll need it to push wood putty into nail holes and gaps in joints.

STEPLADDERS. You'll need one 6-ft. ladder for you and one for your helper. It's time to walk next door and borrow that extra ladder.

TRIM BRUSH. The foam trim for this project comes preprimed, but it will still require primer and finish coats of paint. Get a top-quality trim brush that's about 3 in. wide.

What to Buy

1 | CROWN MOLDING. The molding used in this project is a crown dentil molding that extends $3^{3}/_{8}$ in. across the ceiling and 4 in. down the wall. It comes in 16-ft. lengths. Some foam-molding profiles are available in only one or two lengths. As a result, you may have to buy a bit more than you need.

2 | CONSTRUCTION ADHESIVE. Make sure to get the goop recommended by the molding manufacturer. This construction adhesive comes in caulk-type canisters. You'll need one canister for each 16-ft. length of molding.

3 | NAILS OR SCREWS. Use 8d finish nails to install the molding on gypsum wallboard. If your room has plaster walls, buy $2^{1}/_{2}$-in. trim head screws. Add a cordless drill and a square trim-head screw bit to your tools and gear list.

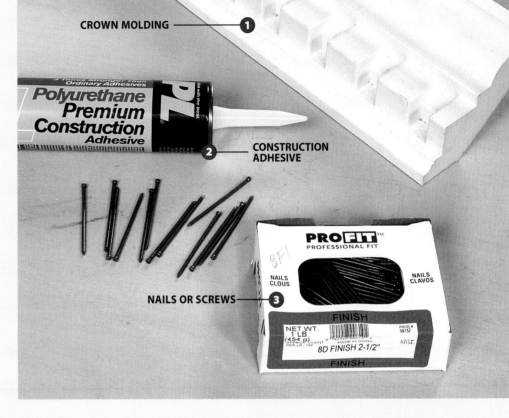

CROWN MOLDING — ①

CONSTRUCTION ADHESIVE — ②

NAILS OR SCREWS — ③

4 | FILLER & CAULK. You will have gaps in molding joints and between the molding and ceiling and wall surfaces. Buy the filler and caulk recommended by the molding manufacturer.

5 | PRIMER & PAINT. Buy a water-based interior primer and a latex semigloss trim paint. Top-quality latex paints say "100% acrylic" on the label.

COOL TOOL

Whether you are using a standard miter box like the one shown here or a motorized version, you can improve your tool by adding a plywood auxiliary fence. The wood fence adds some extra height that is helpful when cutting larger moldings. A piece of $1/2$-in. plywood about 5 in. high and 2 ft. long should do the trick. If your saw has holes in its metal fence, you can drive screws through these holes to mount your auxiliary fence. If not, drill your own holes or mount your auxiliary fence with double-sided tape. Before using the saw, use a square to make sure the fence is at a right angle to the base, and cut through the wooden fence at 45 degrees to the left and 45 degrees to the right.

Making the Cuts

1 **START WITH OUTSIDE CORNER MITERS.** Dentil molding looks best when it turns outside corners with a full dentil. Begin by cutting each piece about 3 in. longer than it needs to be. To cut the right side of the miter, set the blade 45 degrees to your right. Place the molding upside down, extending left of the blade. (Pretend the base of your miter box is the ceiling and the fence is the wall.) Make the cut so it goes through the right front corner of a dentil. Next, swing the blade to the left and cut the mating piece.

2 **MITER THE OPPOSITE ENDS.** If the piece ends midwall, cut it square on the end so the next piece can butt right against it. Otherwise, set up your miter box and molding to make either another outside miter or an inside miter joint at the opposite end of each piece you cut in step 1. Use your sample joints to confirm that the blade is angled the right way. When you're measuring for a miter cut on the opposite end, remember that it's better to cut a piece too long rather than too short.

3 **TEST-FIT, THEN BUTTER UP.** Temporarily tack the pieces you've cut into place by driving finish nails only partway into the wall. Confirm that joints fit together. Then put a squiggly line of construction adhesive on the top and bottom edges that will contact the ceiling and wall. Also put adhesive on outside miter joints.

4 **NAIL IT UP.** Drive 8d nails about every 16 in. Use the same spacing if you're driving trim-head screws into plaster walls and ceilings. Place your fasteners in the thin areas of the molding, not in the dentils. Don't worry if you aren't fastening into studs or ceiling joists. The fasteners just need to hold the molding in place until the adhesive sets.

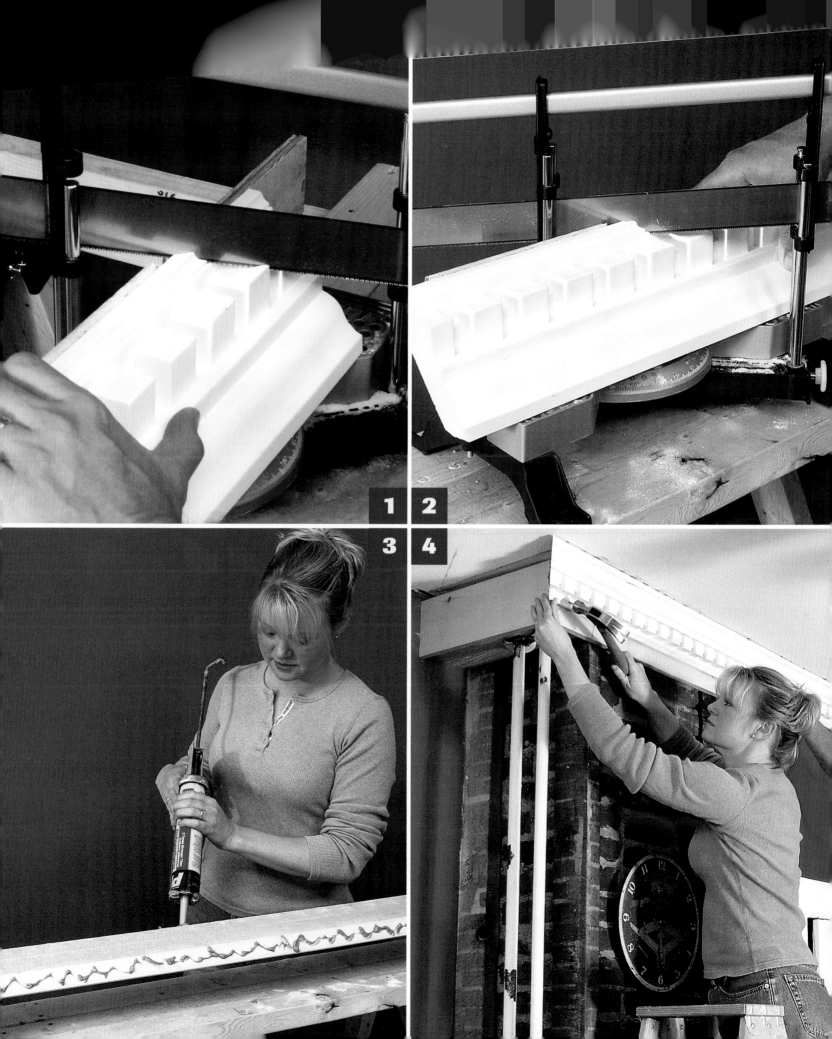

Putting It Up

5 **MARK FOR "MIRROR-IMAGE" INSIDE MITERS.** Just like outside miters, inside miters require symmetrical, "mirror-image" miter cuts to be made in the joining pieces. Measure how much of the dentil detail remains on each inside miter you've already cut and installed. Then transfer this measurement to the molding you need to cut to complete the joint.

6 **CUT INSIDE CORNERS.** To cut the right side of an inside corner, swing the blade 45 degrees to the left and position the molding upside down on the left side of the saw. Do the reverse to cut the right side of an inside miter. Before you make each miter cut, make sure the blade is positioned on the "waste" side of the marks you made in the previous step.

7 **MATCH UP THE BUTT JOINTS.** Where lengths of molding butt together, the dentil pattern needs to remain as uniform as possible. To maintain this uniformity, you'll probably need to square-cut the molding between two corner joints and insert a "right-size" piece to give you correct dentil spacing. Measure, mark, and cut the pieces you need to get the best dentil pattern spacing.

8 **INSTALL REMAINING PIECES, THEN FINISH UP.** Work your way around the room, cutting and installing all remaining pieces of molding. Then set all nails, fill holes with putty, and caulk all gaps between sections of molding and between molding and wall or ceiling surfaces. Smooth rough surfaces and sharp edges with sandpaper, then finish with primer and trim paint.

5

6

7

8

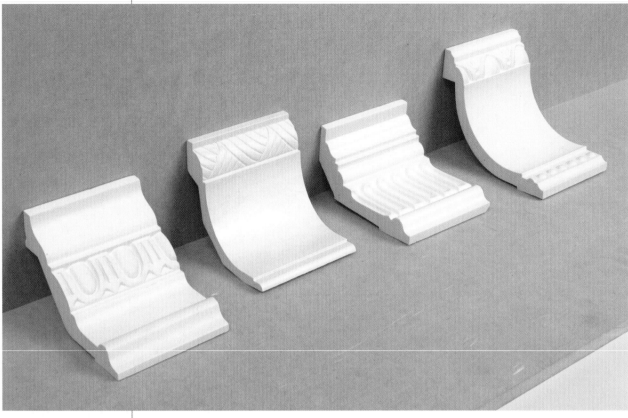

These cross-sections taken from several cornice profiles tell the inside story of plastic's appeal as a molding material. The core is made from foam that's dense but light and dimensionally stable. The outer "show" surface can be formed to include intricate details, and the factory-applied primer provides a smooth base for finish coats of paint.

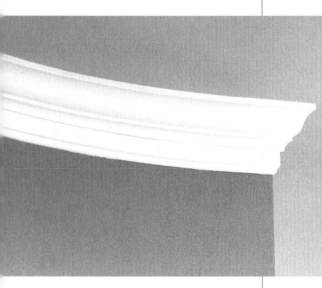

Flexible plastic moldings look like wood or plaster but can bend to fit against curved walls. Available in different profiles, these moldings come preprimed. But don't add finish coats of paint until after the molding is in place.

It's as good as wood, so it's easy to understand why plastic moldings are becoming more and more popular. They're lighter than wood versions, and they don't warp, split, or bow out of shape. Easy to cut and install, these moldings can look just like painted wood or plaster when your installation work is done. You can even get plastic moldings with a factory-applied finish that looks remarkably like real wood. As the selection of plastic moldings grows, so do your design possibilities. Here are a few ideas to get you started.

The cornice in this kitchen proves that two coves are better than one. The small cove in the oak molding used to trim out the top of the wall cabinets is echoed by the cove profile in the larger molding.

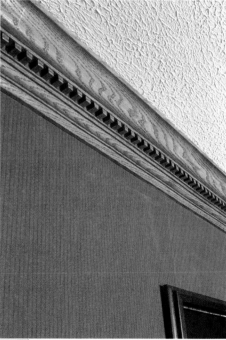

Yes that's plastic! Some urethane molding profiles, including this crown, are available with a surface finish that looks like real wood. You can even stain this molding any color you like as long as you use a nonpenetrating stain.

Mantelpiece

With or without a fireplace, **MITERED MOLDINGS** make this ornate
shelf fit for trophies, trinkets & other treasures

DMIT IT: YOU'VE BEEN ADMIRING these ornate display shelves in your favorite home-furnishing catalogs. But in the time it takes to order a factory-made shelf and get it shipped to your home, you could build and finish several of these shelves yourself. The materials for the shelf shown here will cost you less than $15, so you'll save loads of money. And since you're in charge, you can design mantelpiece shelves in any size and style you like by combining different moldings with the square-edged boards used to make top and bottom pieces. Finish up with your choice of paint, stain, or varnish, and you'll give this project a unique style that can't be found in any catalog.

CUTTING CROWN   GLUE   SAND & FINISH   HANG IT!

✺ DO IT FAST

Planning to finish the shelf differently from the crown? Perhaps an oak shelf with a clear finish or stained and varnished pine? To speed the process, sand and finish the shelf and paint the crown before assembly so you'll just have to touch up at the end.

❖ COOL TOOL

It's called a palm sander because it fits in one hand, leaving the other free to hold the work. Palm sanders take a quarter-sheet of sandpaper and make quick work of jobs like smoothing the shelf. You can even use it to make nicely rounded edges.

Tools & Gear

Keep your basic tool kit handy because you'll need a hammer, tape measure, and nail set.

MITER BOX. To miter the molding you'll need a miter box. A good miter box like the one used in this project comes with its own fine-tooth saw and costs about $40. Avoid cheaper wooden or plastic boxes that have slotted sides. If you want pro-level speed and precision, get a chopsaw (see p. 13).

COMBINATION SQUARE. This adjustable square is a versatile layout tool. For this project, you'll use a combination square to mark where the top of the molding meets the bottom of the shelf board.

DRILL. You'll need one to predrill holes for the hanger screws.

CIRCULAR SAW. You'll need this power saw to cut the shelf board to size. To ensure smooth cuts, make sure you've got a finish-cutting blade in your saw.

PAINTBRUSH & RAGS. Your display shelf deserves a fine finish. A good-quality 3-in. paintbrush is what you need to apply primer and paint or stain and varnish. If you're using oil-base paint or varnish, make sure to use a natural-bristle brush or a synthetic brush recommended for use with oil or alkyd finishes. If your finishing plans involve applying stain or varnish, also get a few clean, soft rags.

DO IT RIGHT

To prep your miter box for the cutting work in this project, anchor the box to a workbench or to sawhorses with some screws. Most miter boxes have holes in the feet or base for screwdown attachment. The other prep step involves attaching a plywood auxiliary fence to your saw's standard fence. A higher fence that you can cut into will help you get more exact cuts in your molding (see COOL TOOL on p.101).

What to Buy

1 | CROWN MOLDING. The molding used for this project is $^9/_{16}$ in. thick and $4^5/_8$ in. wide. You'll find crown molding in different sizes and shapes at your home center or lumberyard. Choose any profile you like as long as the overall width of the molding is at least $3^1/_2$ in. Molding is usually sold by the foot. Get a piece that's straight and at least 1 ft. longer than the planned length of your finished shelf.

2 | 5/4 X 6 PINE. A 5/4 x 6 pine board is really about 1 in. thick and $5^1/_2$ in. wide. Look for a straight, flat, knot-free piece that's as long as you want your shelf to be.

3 | BRADS. These tiny nails are for fastening the molding to the underside of the shelf. Buy a small box of 1-in. brads.

4 | YELLOW GLUE. This woodworking glue will bond the molding pieces to each other and to the shelf. The brads just hold things together until the glue sets.

5 | SANDPAPER. Buy a couple of sheets of 120 grit for rounding the shelf edges and sanding putty patches smooth.

6 | WOOD PUTTY. Make sure you have some putty on hand for filling brad holes and small gaps in joints.

7 | FINISH. For a painted finish, get interior primer and semi-

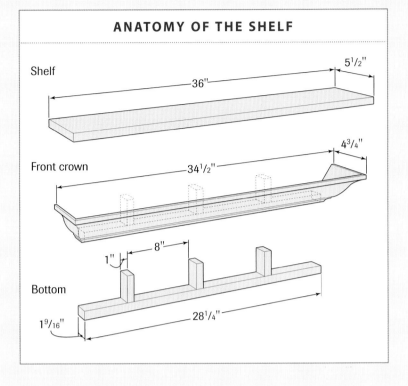

ANATOMY OF THE SHELF

Shelf — 36" — $5^1/_2$"

Front crown — $34^1/_2$" — $4^3/_4$"

Bottom — 1" — 8" — $1^9/_{16}$" — $28^1/_4$"

gloss trim paint. Use polyurethane varnish for a clear finish. Stain or tinted varnish are other finishing options.

8 | FLUSH-MOUNT HARDWARE. One piece of each interlocking pair mounts on the wall; the other is fastened to the back of the finished shelf. You'll need two sets of flush-mount hardware for this project.

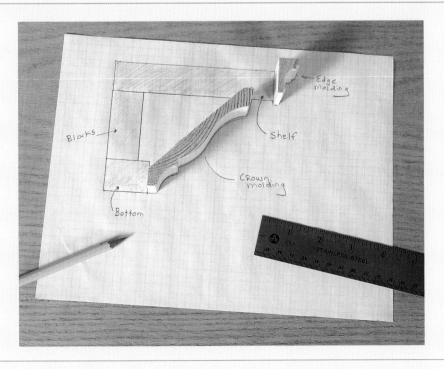

Edge molding

Blocks

Shelf

Crown molding

Bottom

DESIGN YOUR SHELF

You can design a mantelpiece shelf with a single molding or combine different moldings to build up a larger and more elaborate architectural detail. Here's a design strategy that's easy and fun: Using your miter box, slice off an inch or so of the molding or moldings you plan to use. Place these molding cross sections on a piece of graph paper, combining them with the full-scale section drawings of the other parts of your mantelpiece—the shelf, bottom, and backer blocks. This exercise will show you what the completed mantelpiece profile will look like and what the dimensions of the parts need to be.

The proportions of your display shelf will depend on the size of the crown molding you plan to use. To get an exact idea of how high and deep the molding is when it's installed, cut off a small section and place it against a framing square, as shown in the drawing. Now you'll have an easy time determining what the width of the shelf should be.

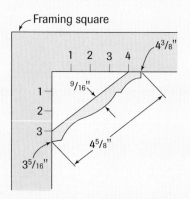

Framing square

Attach the Front Crown

1 **CUT & MARK THE SHELF BOARD.** Using a circular saw, cut the 5/4 x 6 stock to the length you choose—36 in. is shown here. Then decide how far over the crown molding you want the shelf board to extend—¾ in. in this case. Use your combination square to mark the underside of the shelf board, showing where the top edge of each molding piece will fit.

2 **CUT THE FRONT MOLDING PIECE.** Make the miter cut for the left side of the front molding piece. To do this, put the molding upside down on the left side of the saw, and swing the blade 45 degrees to your right. Align the blade with your cut line, and make the cut. Holding the front molding piece in its installed position on the shelf board, mark where the opposite miter needs to be cut. Reverse the setup of your first miter to cut this opposite one.

3 **ATTACH THE FRONT CROWN.** Start 1-in. brads into the molding, orienting them so they will go straight into the bottom of the shelf board. Put yellow glue on the narrow top edge of the molding. Holding the molding in place along your layout line, drive and set the nails.

4 **CUT THE SIDE MOLDING PIECES.** Cut outside miters on the two pieces of molding that join the front piece. Put each piece in place, and mark where they cross the back of the shelf. Square-cut both side pieces to length.

Finish It Up

Prefer the look of natural wood?
If so, you can make your mantelpiece shelf from oak crown molding and an oak shelf board. Both of these ingredients are in stock at most home centers and lumberyards. Finish the project with a couple of coats of polyurethane varnish. Oak is a lot harder than pine, so predrill all your brad and nail holes.

Want to give the edges of your shelf a gentle curve? You can do this by using a block plane. Adjust the blade to take a light cut (you can test this on scrap stock), then plane the ends of the shelf first, followed by the shelf's front edges. You'll still need to complete the smoothing at the shelf edges with sandpaper, but the block plane treatment adds a nice handcrafted touch.

5 **CUT & INSTALL THE BOTTOM PIECE.** Using a circular saw, cut your bottom board to its finished width. Square-cut one end of the board, and hold it in place along the bottom edge of the front molding. Mark it so you can cut it to final length, then make the cut using your miter box. Attach the bottom to the front molding piece with glue and 1-in. brads.

6 **INSTALL SIDE MOLDINGS & BLOCKS.** Attach the side molding pieces with glue and brads. Make sure to spread glue generously on miter joints, then fasten the side pieces to the shelf board and the bottom. To bridge the gap between the shelf board and the bottom, cut three blocks. Space them evenly apart, and install them with glue and 6d finish nails.

7 **FILL, SAND & FINISH.** Fill all nail holes with wood putty; also putty up any gaps between joints. When the filler has hardened, give your shelf a thorough sanding. The shelf edges will look great if you just cup a folded piece of sandpaper in your hands and run it along the top and bottom edges. Apply primer and two coats of trim paint.

8 **HANG IT UP.** Lightly pencil a level line on the wall where you want the top of the shelf to be. Screw your hanger hardware to the back edge of the shelf board and to the wall. Fasten into studs if possible; otherwise, attach hanger brackets to the wall with screws  and drywall anchors. Install your mantelpiece, then collect some treasures and curios to show off on this special shelf.

5 6

7 8

One shelf can have two finishes. The top of this display shelf is a cherry board finished with clear varnish. The molding detail below is painted in an antique blue color.

Building your own mantle-piece gives you the opportunity to get the proportions right. This example fits nicely over the fireplace. Its earth-toned finish was inspired by the brickwork.

The great thing about making your own mantelpiece shelves is that you can custom-design each one to fit a particular space and express your own sense of style. With some mitering mastery and a selection of your favorite molding profiles, the possibilities are limitless. In fact, if you've finished installing the crown molding in a room, you may have enough left over to build a matching shelf or two.

Think of all the uses…displaying your most beautiful candlesticks in the dining room or your favorite perfumes in the powder room. How about two shelves, or even several, perhaps of different lengths, to create a striking display of collectibles in the living room? Or let a plant or two take advantage of a sunny wall by giving them a shelf to perch on.

Who says you need a fireplace? This mantlepiece can overlook a hot bath instead of a hearth. The trim treatment on the bottom of the shelf includes a stock crown molding above a dentil molding. Bringing a green tile from the wall to the paint store ensured a color match for the shelf.

White is right when you want to create a classic appearance, even in a small display shelf. Use the same molding detail to build shelves in different sizes—this gives you plenty of possibilities for creating a unique wallscape.

Resources

ROBERT BOSCH
POWER TOOL CORP.
S-B Power Tool Co.
4300 W. Petersen Ave.
Chicago, IL 60646
(312) 286-7330
www.boschtools.com

CST/BERGER
(Makers of LaserMark)
P.O. Box 359
255 West Fleming St.
Watseka, IL 60970
(800) 435-1859
(815) 432-5237
www.cstsurvey.com

DEWALT INDUSTRIAL
TOOL CO.
701 East Joppa Rd.
Baltimore, MD 212866
(410) 665-7400
www.DEWALT.com

PORTER-CABLE CORP.
4825 Hwy. 45 North
P.O. Box 2468
Jackson, TN 38302-2468
(800) 487-8665
www.porter-cable.com

STANLEY TOOLS
Division of Stanley Works
1000 Stanley Dr.
New Britian, CT 06053
(860) 225-5111
www.stanleyworks.com

STYLE SOLUTIONS, INC.
(polyurethane crown molding)
960 West Barre Rd.
Archbold, OH 43502
(800) 446-3040
www.stylesolutionsinc.com

Photo Credits

All photos appearing in this book are by Stephen Carver, except:

p. 5: © Randy O'Rourke
p. 25: © Randy O'Rourke
p. 32 (right) © Christian Korab
p. 33 (left) © Randy O'Rourke
p. 35: © Randy O'Rourke
p. 42: (left) © Style Solutions; (right) © Randy O'Rourke
p. 43: (left) © Randy O'Rourke; (top right) sreed@ornamental.com
p. 45: © Randy O'Rourke
p. 52: © davidduncanlivingston.com
p. 53: (left) © Style Solutions; (top right) Photo by Tom O'Brien, courtesy *Fine Homebuilding*, © The Taunton Press, Inc.; (bottom right) © davidduncanlivingston.com
p. 55: © Randy O'Rourke
p. 62: (bottom left) Photo by Andy Engel, courtesy *Fine Homebuilding*, © The Taunton Press, Inc.; (top) Photo by Tom O'Brien, courtesy *Fine Homebuilding*, © The Taunton Press, Inc.
p. 63: (top left) Photo by Jefferson Kolle, courtesy *Fine Homebuilding*, © The Taunton Press, Inc.; (top right) Photo by Scott Gibson, courtesy *Fine Homebuilding*, © The Taunton Press, Inc.
p. 65: © Randy O'Rourke
p. 72: (left) Photo by Andy Engel, courtesy *Fine Homebuilding*, © The Taunton Press, Inc.; (right) Photo by Scott Gibson, courtesy *Fine Homebuilding*, © The Taunton Press, Inc.
p. 73 (left) Photo by Charles Miller, courtesy *Fine Homebuilding*, © The Taunton Press, Inc.
p. 75: © Randy O'Rourke
p. 84: (top left) sreed@ornamental.com; (bottom left) © Randy O'Rourke; (top right) Photo by Charles Miller, courtesy *Fine Homebuilding*, © The Taunton Press, Inc.; (bottom right) sreed@ornamental.com
p. 85: © Randy O'Rourke
p. 87: © Randy O'Rourke
p. 96: (left top and bottom) © 2004 Georgia Pacific; (right) © Michael Jensen
p. 97: (top left) courtesy *Fine Homebuilding*, © The Taunton Press, Inc.; (bottom left) sreed@ornamental.com; (right) Photo by Kevin Ireton, courtesy *Fine Homebuilding*, © The Taunton Press, Inc.
p. 99: © Randy O'Rourke
p. 106: (top) © Randy O'Rourke; (bottom left) © Style Solutions
p. 107 (left) © Randy O'Rourke; (right) © Style Solutions
p. 108: © Randy O'Rourke
p. 116: (top) © Randy O'Rourke; (bottom left) Photo by Roe A. Osborn, courtesy *Fine Homebuilding*, © The Taunton Press, Inc.
p. 117: © Randy O'Rourke

For more great weekend project ideas look for these and other
TAUNTON PRESS BOOKS wherever books are sold.

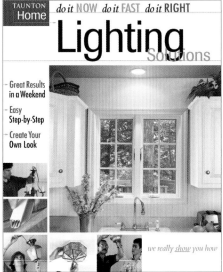

Paint Transformations
1-56158-670-6
Product #070751
$14.95

Lighting Solutions
1-56158-669-2
Product #070753
$14.95

Storage Solutions
1-56158-668-4
Product #070754
$14.95

For more information visit our Web site at www.doitnowfastright.com